SOCIAL WORK AFTER THE AMERICANS WITH DISABILITIES ACT

SOCIAL WORK AFTER THE AMERICANS WITH DISABILITIES ACT

New Challenges and Opportunities for Social Service Professionals

John T. Pardeck

AUBURN HOUSE
Westport, Connecticut • London

Library of Congress Cataloging-in-Publication Data

Pardeck, John T.
    Social work after the Americans with Disabilities Act : new
challenges and opportunities for social service professionals / John
T. Pardeck
        p.   cm.
    Includes bibliographical references and index.
    ISBN 0–86569–265–3 (alk. paper).—ISBN 0–86569–277–7 (pbk. :
alk. paper)
    1. Social work with the handicapped—United States.   2. United
States. Americans with Disabilities Act of 1990.   3. Handicapped—
Civil rights —United States.   I. Title.
HV1553.P37   1998
362.4′0453′0973—dc21   97–50078

British Library Cataloguing in Publication Data is available.

Library of Congress Catalog Card Number: 97–50078
ISBN: 0–86569–265–3
      0–86569–277–7 (pbk.)

First published in 1998

Auburn House, 88 Post Road West, Westport, CT 06881
An imprint of Greenwood Publishing Group, Inc.

Printed in the United States of America

The paper used in this book complies with the
Permanent Paper Standard issued by the National
Information Standards Organization (Z39.48–1984).

10 9 8 7 6 5 4 3 2 1

This book is dedicated to Daniel L. Scholz

Contents

Preface

The goal of this book is to inform social workers and others working in the human services about the mandates and requirements of the Americans With Disabilities Act (ADA). The ADA is considered the "emancipation proclamation" for people with disabilities. The ADA's ultimate meaning is that people with disabilities have finally been written into the U.S. Constitution.

Given the fact that the ADA is the most important civil rights legislation of the 1990s, this new law has profound implications for social workers in all practice settings including higher education. Professional social workers must know the requirements under the ADA because 43 million Americans fall under the act's protection. Many of the clients whom social workers provide services to are protected by the ADA. Numerous professional social workers with disabilities also have new rights under the ADA.

The first chapter of the book introduces the reader to the ADA. An important objective of this chapter is to provide a historical overview of various philosophies that have guided humankind's understanding and treatment of people with disabilities throughout the ages. It is stressed in Chapter 1 that in the United States a more positive view and attitude toward people with disabilities is only a recent phenomenon. Chapter 1 also offers the definition for a disability under the ADA. The major titles of the law are presented. Chapter 2 provides detailed technical information on Title I (employment) and Chapter 3 presents in-depth material on Title II (state and local government). These two titles are the most important components of the ADA for professional social workers regardless of practice setting. Given the titles' importance, entire chapters are dedicated to each one.

Chapter 2 offers the technical components of Title I. Included are examples of the rights of people with disabilities in all aspects of employment. Strategies for minimizing the chances of employment discrimination are stressed in Chapter 2. Chapter 2 reports that over 70,000 discrimination complaints have been filed with the Equal Employment Opportunity Commission (EEOC) under the ADA up to the fall of 1996; a discussion concerning the nature of these complaints is presented. Information is also offered on how the complaints have been resolved. Chapter 5 provides greater detail on strategies that social work agencies can use for preventing and defending employment discrimination complaints under the ADA.

Chapter 3 provides the technical aspects of Title II (state and local government). Title II prohibits discrimination against persons with disabilities in all services, programs, and activities provided or made available by state and local government. The reader will find that Title II is similar to Section 504 of the Rehabilitation Act of 1973. Section 504 protects persons with disabilities from discrimination in public and private entities that receive a certain level of funding from the federal government. If a social work agency is in compliance with Section 504, it probably meets most of the requirements of Title II of the ADA. Professional social workers will find the information in Chapter 3 helpful because it stresses that public agencies cannot discriminate against clients with disabilities in any aspect of service or program delivery. Social workers practicing in educational settings must realize that the same requirements concerning discrimination under Title II hold true for students with disabilities receiving their education in public institutions. Also offered is a brief discussion on Title III (public accommodations). Title III is very similar to Title II; however, it covers private entities such as for-profit social work agencies.

Chapter 4 focuses on the impact the ADA has on social work agencies. This chapter emphasizes that agencies must follow the employment provisions of Title I if they employ fifteen or more people. It also stresses that public social work agencies must follow the mandates under Title II (state and local government). This chapter offers the rights of employees with disabilities in social work agencies as well as the rights of clients with disabilities. An example of an employment discrimination case is presented. Included is a detailed discussion of the legal defenses for alleged job discrimination under the ADA.

Educational issues and the ADA are covered in Chapter 5. The major focus of this chapter is on the rights of students with disabilities at all levels of public and private education. One of the basic rights of students with disabilities is the right to modifications of educational programs to accommodate their disabilities. Under the ADA, students with disabilities can receive this kind of reasonable accommodation if it does not significantly alter an educational program or create an undue hardship. The right of students with disabilities to program modifications applies to all grade levels from primary to graduate school. Chapter 5 places particular emphasis on the ADA requirements that must be followed when screening students for admission to professional social work educational programs. Virtually the same standards that an employer must follow when interviewing a job applicant apply to the screening process for admission to professional social work education. For example, an employer interviewing a job applicant cannot ask any questions about an applicant's health; this requirement is mandated for those involved in the admissions process to professional social work education. Chapter 5 provides critical information on the ADA for professional social workers in every practice setting.

Chapters 6 and 7 cover the topics of advocacy and future issues related to the ADA. Chapter 6 offers an overview of the advocacy process and suggests advocacy strategies for people with disabilities. Chapter 7 concludes that a number of aspects of the ADA are very difficult for some to understand, including the unique definition for a disability under the act. This chapter also emphasizes that training in the ADA is particularly critical for people in the workplace. The book concludes with an appendix, which offers a brief summary of the ADA. This information is provided as an easy guide to the act.

The goal of this book is to inform social workers about the tremendous implications that the ADA has on professional behavior regardless of practice settings. Social workers, like others in American society, must change their attitudes toward people with disabilities. The most significant attitudinal change that must be made by professional social workers is to begin to view people with disabilities as the largest minority group in American society that has finally been written into the U.S. Constitution.

The author appreciates the encouragement of Jean Pardeck, Ruth Pardeck, Lois Musick, and Burl Musick. They all provided help during the preparation of this book.

SOCIAL WORK AFTER THE AMERICANS WITH DISABILITIES ACT

Chapter 1

An Introduction to the Americans With Disabilities Act

On July 26, 1990, President Bush signed the Americans With Disabilities Act (ADA) into law. This legislation is referred to as the "emancipation proclamation for the disabled" because of its great importance to the 43 million Americans with disabilities. These disabilities span a broad spectrum of types and severity. The ADA has significant implications for all citizens, not only those with disabilities. The ADA also has significance for the ways that social work agencies and other systems operate. For example, in local governments, changes have been required in countless ordinances, building codes and policies. Public social work agencies must also make these changes. For private industry, including the for-profit social work agencies, many changes have been required for compliance with the ADA. These include hiring procedures, job restructuring, work schedules, training materials and equipment used, and other factors affecting persons with disabilities working in or coming in contact with the private sector. In essence, the ADA has profound implications for all aspects of American life, including the profession of social work.

Before outlining the reasons for the ADA, and its key provisions, one must understand that social policies with respect to disabled persons are the result of historical processes. These historical processes have been guided by three general philosophies—utilitarianism, humanitarianism, and human rights.

Each of these views developed during different historical eras and reflects the thinking of each era. Each philosophy continues to influence social policy affecting people with disabilities. Thus today we have three philosophies that interact to influence social policy toward Americans with disabilities.

UTILITARIANISM

The central theme of utilitarianism is that usefulness determines the value of a person or thing to society (Sussman, 1965). The utility of a person or thing is relative to each given society; however, the core criterion for usefulness has always been the greatest good or happiness for the greatest number in society. Usefulness had a different meaning among primitive societies compared with modern societies. In primitive societies, the disabled person was often seen as a burden to the social group because he or she could not contribute to the welfare of the group. During times of severe hardship, the disabled were simply abandoned or killed. Even though the expression of the utilitarian philosophy among many primitive societies was barbaric and cruel, it was regarded by those cultures as a necessity for survival (Pardeck and Chung, 1992).

Primitive societies had a very limited view of the world. They viewed disability as the work of evil spirits and supernatural forces as an expression of the disfavor of the gods. The disabled were often seen as a hazard to primitive societies and were thus sacrificed to appease the gods (Brothwell and Sandison, 1967; Galdston, 1963). These beliefs about the disabled persisted into the Middle Ages (Newman, 1987).

The early centuries of Christianity brought about possibilities for improved treatment of the disabled; however, in practice little was done. Even into the medieval age, disabilities were viewed as a consequence of original sin and a sign of God's disfavor. Individuals were seen in terms of good and evil; the disabled were largely viewed as evil (Newman, 1987). Yet within this primitive world there was ambiguity of regard for the disabled, particularly for malformed infants who were preserved and worshipped as awe-inspiring objects (Fiedler, 1978). Such ambiguities are seen as the basis of present-day conflictual attitudes toward disabilities, which all too frequently result in policies of isolation, segregation, and discrimination (Gellman, 1959; Galdston, 1963).

HUMANITARIANISM

During the Renaissance, the Church established a new view that all life was sacred. However, the principal focus of early Christian doctrine on a future heavenly life, rather than present earthly one, did not lead to significant change in the treatment of the disabled. However, the nascent forces were created during the Renaissance that evolved into the philosophy of humanitarianism. This philosophy attached central importance to the well-being of all people. That is, each person has worth and is not subordinated to political and biological theories. Given this progressive view, new thought in all fields began to emerge. Politics, arts, literature, architecture and science saw individuals from a new perspective. The core principles of humanistic philosophy evolved from these fields (Newman, 1987).

Unfortunately, during the Renaissance, most persons with disabilities did not survive to adulthood. Furthermore, Western societies had neither the infrastructure nor the capabilities and resources to cope with the overwhelming number of people with disabilities. These conditions would not begin to change until the latter half of the nineteenth century. Gradually the growth of wealth in Western societies led to advanced knowledge and technology; these changes stirred efforts to change society in ways that would mitigate the harshness of the utilitarian philosophy. Out of these conditions grew the humanitarian movement (Newman, 1987).

Along with the humanitarian treatment of the disabled in the nineteenth century, a conflicting view, Social Darwinism, was also emerging. Social Darwinism often resulted in indifference toward the disabled. The disabled were simply viewed as unfit, and thus not caring for the disabled was justified under the tenets of this philosophy. The principal beliefs of eugenicists emerged from Social Darwinism. For disabled persons, eugenicists advocated euthanasia, prohibition of marriage, segregation, and sterilization (Newman, 1987).

Legislation toward these ends began in 1897, and by the 1930s, twenty-eight states had sterilization laws (Burgdorf and Burgdorf, 1977). Laws banning the disabled from appearing in public were also common in the early 1900s (Ianacone, 1977). For example, in 1900, Chicago had a municipal ordinance called "The Ugly Law" that barred disabled people from appearing on the streets. In 1919, a Wisconsin school board expelled a student with cerebral palsy, even though he was keeping up with the class, because the students and school personnel found the student repulsive (*Governmental Affairs Newsletter*, 1991).

Many of the punitive laws concerning the disabled were challenged as unconstitutional. One notable case, *Buck v. Bell*, reached the Supreme Court in 1927. The Supreme Court found the law challenged in *Buck v. Bell* to be constitutional, thus making it legal to sterilize the mentally disabled. However, *Buck v. Bell* was one of many cases that were ultimately challenged within the legal system (Hull, 1977).

Into the twentieth century, caring for the disabled was largely viewed as a problem relegated to private humanitarian groups. The groups' focus was largely on the creation of institutions to care for the disadvantaged. Such institutional treatment posed numerous problems, including negative psychological and social effects resulting from such custodial institutions for the disabled. It was becoming apparent that the power and resources of government must be involved to correct the limited efforts by private humanitarian groups, and in particular the negative effects of Social Darwinism (Newman, 1987).

HUMAN RIGHTS PHILOSOPHY

The philosophy of human rights is reflected through law, specifically in the Constitution, the Bill of Rights, and the fifth and fourteenth Amendments to the Constitution, which guarantee rights, equal protection, and due process. The human rights philosophy has elements of the humanitarian philosophy with its emphasis on the intrinsic value of the individual. What separates the humanitarian philosophy from the human rights view, however, is the fact that the intrinsic worth of the individual is protected by law. In the United States, this protection is found in the Constitution (Newman, 1987).

Human rights for people with disabilities were influenced by allied movements for civil and minority rights. As in the minority rights struggle, the focus was largely on the right to a public education. Public education for the child with a disability was limited, and most were excluded from the mainstream education environment. The challenge to this exclusion began with the *Brown v. Board of Education* case on behalf of black children (Fiedler, 1978). The decision, handed down in 1954, was grounded in the Fourteenth Amendment, which guarantees all people equal protection under the law. Under this law, what is done to some people must be done to all persons on equal terms unless a compelling cause for differential treatment can be shown. Thus the rationale for equal educational opportunity was established for all. The state cannot set up separate systems and procedures for dealing with different persons (Newman, 1987). The child with a disability has a right to the same education received by other children (Hull, 1977).

Legal efforts in earlier years helped to establish the present-day movements for deinstitutionalization and integration of people with disabilities into the larger society. The authority for these influenced three major pieces of federal legislation in the 1970s: (1) Education for All Handicapped

Children Act (P.L. 94–142, 1975); (2) Title V (Section 504), Rehabilitation Amendments of 1973 (P.L. 93–112); and (3) the Developmentally Disabled Assistance and Bill of Rights Act (P.L. 94–103, 1975). All three pieces of legislation are grounded in the human rights philosophy and essentially afforded these statutory safeguards: (1) accessibility to facilities and programs supported by or operated by the federal government; (2) protection against discrimination in federally assisted programs; and (3) the right to a free, appropriate education (Newman, 1987).

THE AMERICANS WITH DISABILITIES ACT

The ADA is grounded in the human rights philosophy. It is based on the position that persons with disabilities have not received the same treatment as others, and that it is the responsibility of the state to affirm or reaffirm those rights through judicial and legislative actions. The humanitarian philosophy also comes through in the ADA because people with disabilities are viewed as having intrinsic worth and dignity. But utilitarian factors also have limited influence on the ADA; for example, employers must make reasonable accommodations to assist the person with a disability in the workplace. The cost of accommodating the person with a disability cannot necessarily outweigh the benefits. The utilitarian view always stresses the practicality and cost-effectiveness of programs.

Findings Supporting Need for the ADA

The ADA (P.L. Law 101–336, 1990) was signed into law based on the following findings:

1. There are 43 million Americans who have one or more physical or mental disabilities.

2. Historically, society has tended to isolate and segregate the disabled.

3. Discrimination in employment, housing, public accommodations, transportation, and education has been an enormous deterrent in the implementation of the rights of the disabled.

4. Discrimination on the basis of disability frequently had no legal recourse.

5. Individuals with disabilities are intentionally excluded by architectural, transportation, or communication barriers, and practices that result in fewer opportunities.

6. People with disabilities as a group occupy inferior status and are disadvantaged socially, vocationally, economically, and educationally.

7. Individuals with disabilities are a distinct and insular minority who have been faced with restrictions and limitations and subjected to unequal treatment.

8. The nation's goals should be to ensure equality of opportunity, full participation, independent living, and economic self-sufficiency.

9. The continued existence of unfair and unnecessary discrimination against the disabled denies opportunity to compete, and costs the United States billions of dollars in unnecessary expenses resulting from dependency and nonproductivity.

Purposes of the ADA

There are four purposes of the ADA based on the nine findings:

1. To provide a national mandate to eliminate discrimination against individuals with disabilities.

2. To provide an enforceable standard addressing discrimination.

3. To ensure that the federal government will play a central role in enforcing these standards.

4. To involve congressional authority in order to address the major areas of discrimination faced by people with disabilities.

There are five major titles under the ADA. The definition of disability established in the Rehabilitation Act of 1973 was adopted in the ADA. In this definition, disability means a physical or mental impairment that substantially limits one or more of the major life activities of an individual, a record of such an impairment, or being regarded as having such an impairment.

Under this definition, disabilities include the following: mobility impairments, sensory impairments, mental retardation, and hidden disabilities such as cancer, diabetes, epilepsy, heart disease and mental illness. Individuals who have a history of these disabilities but are no longer disabled, or who have been incorrectly classified as having a disability, or who do not have a disability but who are treated or perceived by others as having a disability are protected by the ADA.

Major Titles of the ADA

Title I: Discrimination Regarding Employment. This title defines and describes how employers are prohibited from discriminating against a qualified individual with a disability in all terms and conditions of employment. This title has the greatest importance for employee selection.

Title II: Public Services. This title prohibits discrimination and increases the accessibility of persons with disabilities to programs run by state and local governments. In the field of social work this includes public social work agencies, colleges, and universities. This title also requires public transportation to be accessible to people with disabilities.

Title III: Private Accommodations and Services. This title requires that private businesses serving the public make their goods and services available to people with disabilities.

Title IV: Telecommunications. This title requires that telephone services be accessible to people with hearing and speech impairments by providing them with relay services. The relay service uses an operator as an intermediary communicator between the hearing person and the individual needing assistance.

Title V: Miscellaneous. This title prohibits retaliation against an individual because of actions related to the act, and provides information on the implementation of the ADA, the Rehabilitation Act of 1973, and state laws.

Title I (Employment)

The Rehabilitation Act of 1973 was the first significant national legislation to protect people with disabilities. The Rehabilitation Act, however, covers only those entities that receive federal contracts or subcontracts exceeding a certain dollar amount. The Rehabilitation Act served as the model for the Americans With Disabilities Act including Title I of the ADA.

Title I of the ADA covers all employers, public and private, who employ fifteen or more workers. Since employment discrimination has long been a problem for people with disabilities, the goal of Title I is to prevent this kind of discrimination.

Discrimination against people with disabilities occurs in many different forms in the workplace. Some of the discrimination is intentional; some is unintentional. Much of the discrimination against people with disabilities is a result of able people who see the disabled as different from others. The media have portrayed people with disabilities as different, and often this portrayal is extreme. For example, some people with disabilities are viewed as extremely dependent; others are presented as superheroes such as Ironside from the famous television series about the lawyer who used a wheelchair. These extremes are often unrealistic and do not help the able better understand people with disabilities. As children, people often experienced educational systems that segregated people with disabilities from others. This kind of segregation also extended into the workplace, for example, the placement of persons with disabilities in Sheltered Workshops. This kind of separation has increased our lack of awareness of people with disabilities and their special needs. Segregation of people with disabilities from the able emphasizes the differences of people in the two groups and not their similarities. Segregation of people with disabilities in schools and the workplace has increased able persons' fears and discomfort with people who have disabilities.

Title I of the ADA is aimed at changing the historical patterns of excluding people with disabilities from the workplace. The objective of Title I is to place people with disabilities in meaningful employment and to offer them job opportunities that nondisabled people take for granted. Once people with disabilities have achieved greater integration into the workplace, many of the misconceptions about people with disabilities will be eliminated.

To comply with Title I, employers must make sure that the employee selection process is clearly understood by all employees. The requirements of the ADA in employment must be provided to all employees. Employers must understand that the employment provisions of the ADA cover hiring, promotions, pay, firing, job training, benefits—virtually all aspects of the workplace. National legislators recognized that they could not predict every possible form of employment discrimination, so they created a law that is broad and open to interpretation. An important component of Title I is defining who is protected and outlining the basic responsibilities of employers.

Employers must understand that Title I includes a definition not only of a disability but also for what is meant by a qualified individual with a disability. A qualified individual with a disability under the employment provisions of the ADA is as follows (Equal Employment Opportunity Commission and U.S. Department of Justice, 1992:2):

A qualified individual with a disability is a person who meets legitimate skill, experience, education, or other requirements of an employment position that s/he holds or seeks, and who can perform the "essential" functions of the position with or without reasonable accommodation. Requiring the ability to perform "essential" functions assures that an individual with a disability will not be considered unqualified simply because of inability to perform marginal or incidental job functions.

If an individual is qualified to perform essential job functions except for limitations caused by a disability, the employer must consider whether the individual could perform these functions with a reasonable accommodation. If a written job description has been prepared in advance of advertising or interviewing applicants for a job, this will be considered as evidence, although not conclusive evidence, of the essential functions of the job.

Essential functions of a job include the fundamental duties required of a position. These qualifications include educational requirements, work experience, training levels, job skills, licensing and certification requirements, and other job-related requirements determined by the employer.

Even though the ADA does not mandate it, employers should have a complete job description for all positions in an organization including those that the employer wishes to fill. The essential function of a job is the primary responsibilities of the position. Employers should list in writing any key duties for a position; these should become a part of the job description. Title I does not require employers to eliminate or make changes to core job duties or essential functions of the job for the person with a disability. However, every position typically has several tasks that are not vital to the position; these kinds of tasks are viewed as nonessential functions. Under the ADA, an employer cannot refuse to hire people with a disability because of their inability to do a nonessential task.

Title I emphasizes that an organization has every right to hire the most qualified individual. Obviously, the most qualified individual is the one who can best perform the essential functions of the job, with or without accommodations. It is the employer's responsibility to determine these essential functions. Employers should be prepared, however, to provide reasonable accommodations to help the person with a disability perform a job.

Essential functions of a job are related to the definition of a qualified individual with a disability. A qualified person with a disability is one who meets all of the qualifications of a job, including but not limited to educational requirements, work experience, training skills, and licensing and certification requirements. If a person with a disability applies for a position, an employer must determine if these essential functions can be performed with or without reasonable accommodations. When considering individuals for a position, it is critical for the employer to apply hiring criteria consistently to all applicants, including the able and persons with disabilities. If a person with a disability is the most qualified person for a position, that person should be offered the position. This is equally true for the able person.

Reasonable accommodation is an important aspect of Title I as well as of other titles under the ADA. A reasonable accommodation is a modification or adjustment for a position that helps a qualified individual with a disability perform the tasks of a job. The employer can accommodate both the essential functions and the nonessential functions of a position.

Title I suggests that reasonable accommodations can be made under the following situations:

1. During the job application process, including the job interview.

2. Helping employees with disabilities enjoy equal benefits and privileges of employment.

3. Helping employees with disabilities perform the essential functions of a position.

During the job application process, for example, reasonable accommodations may be offered to an applicant to ensure equal opportunity. For example, a social work agency may offer the hearing-impaired person an interpreter during the interview. A hearing impairment does not automatically mean the person does not qualify for a position.

Reasonable accommodations take many forms. The following are examples of reasonable accommodations that have relevance to the social work agency:

1. A social work agency must be readily accessible to and usable by people with disabilities. An example of this is creating a work station for a person using a chair that has an adjusted desktop to help the employee reach objects on the desk and files.

2. Modifying the essential functions of a position is also a reasonable accommodation. In a social work agency, this might entail providing the individual with a hand impairment with a computer keyboard designed for use with this kind of impairment.

3. An agency may also wish to reassign the nonessential functions of a position to others. For example, a nonessential function of a clerical position may be the distribution of memos within the agency. This responsibility may be assigned to an able person who can easily perform these functions.

4. The modification of an employee's work schedule is another strategy that can be used to accommodate the worker with a disability. If a worker within the agency must go for weekly treatments for cancer, for example, the agency can require the employee to make up the missed time during the evening or weekends.

5. Agencies often require examinations and training. The hearing-impaired employee may need these examinations and training materials in written script that corresponds, for example, to a video that is used during a training session. An employee with a learning disability may require that an agency examination be read aloud. Such an employee may also be given a longer testing period. Chapter 5 emphasizes that this kind of reasonable accommodation may also be required of social work programs educating the special-needs student.

6. Social work agencies must also ensure that persons with disabilities have equal access to all employee benefits and to other privileges of employment. For example, an agency cannot require only people with disabilities to take a medical exam. A lunchroom, for example, must be accessible to all in an agency, including people with disabilities. In fact, a reasonable accommodation might be moving the lunchroom to an accessible area for a person with a disability.

The possibilities are endless for providing reasonable accommodations to people with disabilities in the workplace. It must be remembered that there is not just one solution for every disability.

One final aspect of Title I of the ADA is that an employer can refuse to hire an otherwise qualified individual with a disability if that person requires an accommodation that would result in an undue hardship for the employer. In other words, the accommodation that is requested by the person with a disability may be unreasonable. Undue hardship might result from:

1. The nature and net cost of the accommodation.

2. The financial resources that the social work agency has, including the number of workers employed, and the effect the accommodation would have on agency resources.

3. The impact the accommodation has on other workers. If the requested accommodation makes it difficult for other employees to perform their jobs, the accommodation would be seen as unreasonable.

The larger the social work agency and the greater its financial resources, the more difficult it is to prove that an accommodation is an undue hardship. When an agency denies an accommodation because it is viewed as an undue hardship, the agency must be able to prove its case even in a court of law.

Title I Sample Case

The first ADA case that the EEOC took to federal court was *EEOC v. AIC Security Investigations* (1993). Compensatory and punitive damages were awarded under this case. The complainant, Charles L. Wessel, was an executive director of the security guard division of AIC Security Investigations in Chicago, IL. His was the highest management position in the company. The essential functions of Wessel's position included the management of 300 employees, dealing with labor unions, supervising investigations and other matters. Wessel was highly regarded in the security industry (Spencer, 1995).

In June 1987, the complainant was diagnosed with lung cancer. Following treatment, he returned to work at AIC. He had additional cancer treatment in July 1991; after recuperation he again returned to work. In April 1992, Wessel was diagnosed with four inoperable brain tumors and was told he had no more than twelve months to live. He did, however, go for additional treatment to control the tumors (Spencer, 1995).

The complainant continued to work at AIC throughout the course of his treatments. He took half days off for treatments. In July 1992, Wessel was told he had to retire. Prior to his forced retirement, he never received warnings related to his job performance or his attendance (Spencer, 1995).

After his forced retirement, Wessel filed a complaint with the EEOC. The EEOC sued AIC for job discrimination under Title I of the ADA. AIC responded that although the complainant was clearly an individual with a disability, he was not a "qualified individual with a disability" and therefore was not covered under Title I. To support its claim, AIC argued that the complainant's absence and short-term memory loss interfered with his ability to perform the essential tasks of his job, even when reasonable accommodations were provided. As mentioned earlier, if an employee cannot perform the essential functions of a position, he or she is not "otherwise qualified" for the position under Title I (Spencer, 1995).

The EEOC presented evidence that the complainant's absences were no different from absences taken by other employees at AIC who had treatment for other illnesses. Wessel also was able to maintain a high level of customer contact and no complaints had been made concerning his performance. The EEOC also argued that the evidence did not establish that Wessel's short-term memory lapses interfered with his job performance or that he was unable to do the essential functions of his job. AIC's own expert argued that if short-term memory loss were a problem, it could be reasonably accommodated by Wessel's keeping notes and writing things down. The issues of whether his work attendance or his short-term memory losses prevented him from performing the essential functions of his job were presented to the jury; the jury returned a verdict for Wessel and the EEOC. The court judgment against AIC and the sole owner of the company included the following (Spencer, 1995):

1. AIC was ordered to pay $22,000 in back pay from the time the complainant was terminated through the time he began experiencing seizures, which would have prevented him from working.

2. AIC had to pay $50,000 in compensatory damages, based on the jury award.

3. AIC was ordered to pay $150,000 in punitive damages, reduced from the jury award of $500,000, which exceeded the combined limit for compensatory and punitive damages under Title I of the ADA.

4. Equitable relief, which included an injunction prohibiting defendants from engaging in employment practices that discriminate against any qualified person on the basis of disability, an injunction prohibiting retaliation, a requirement that defendants provide notice of the lawsuit to all employees, and that AIC maintain records of employees with disabilities available for inspection by the EEOC.

Title II (Public Services)

This title of the ADA prohibits discrimination against persons with disabilities in all services, programs, and activities provided or made available by state or local government. Many state and local governments were prohibited from discriminating against persons with disabilities prior to the ADA under Section 504 of the Rehabilitation Act of 1973.

Section 504 prohibits discrimination on the basis of disability in any programs and activities that receive a set amount of federal funds. Title II of the ADA extends the nondiscrimination requirements of Section 504 to the activities of all state and local governments, regardless of whether they receive federal support. Title II has two subtitles: Subtitle A covers all activities of state and local governments other than public transit, and Subtitle B deals with the provision of publicly funded transit.

Activities Covered Under Title II

Title II covers every type of state or local government activity or program. In employment, state and local governments cannot discriminate against job applicants and employees with disabilities regardless of the number of people they employ.

Title II also covers the following (Equal Employment Opportunity Commission and U.S. Department of Justice, 1992):

1. Activities and programs involving general public contact, including communication with the public through telephone contact, office walk-ins, and interviews.

2. Activities and programs directly administered by state and local governments for beneficiaries and participants, including programs that provide state or local government services and benefits.

Examples of activities covered under Title II include voting, jury duty, town meetings, board meetings, licensure and registration, and the administration of public benefits including social services. Title II also covers public school systems' programs and activities. Activities that must be made available to people with disabilities including students are graduation ceremonies, parent-teacher organization meetings, plays, classroom activities, and adult education.

Under Title II, a person must be a "qualified individual with a disability" in order to be protected. A qualified individual with a disability is defined as a person who—with or without reasonable modifications to rules, policies, and practices—meets the essential eligibility requirements for the receipt of services or the participation in programs or activities provided by a state or local government (Equal Employment Opportunity Commission and U.S. Department of Justice, 1992). A state or local government must document that an eligibility requirement is essential before it can conclude that a person with a disability is unable to meet the essential eligibility requirements. It must also consider whether the person with a disability can meet basic eligibility requirements if modifications can be made such as (1) modifying rules, policies, or practice; (2) removing architectural or transportation barriers; and (3) providing auxiliary aids and services. If such measures enable a person with a disability to meet essential eligibility requirements, the person is a "qualified individual with a disability."

Subtitle A of Title II has a number of basic requirements critical to social service agencies in the public sector. These also apply to all activities of state or local government. Furthermore, if a state or local government enters into a contract with a private entity, it must ensure that the activity operated under contract is in compliance with Title II. Compliance for the private entity extends only to the activity that is the subject of the contract. The following are some of the basic requirements under Title I, Subtitle A (Great Plains Disability and Business Technical Assistance Center, 1995):

1. Integrated Setting. Integration is the fundamental component of Title II. State or local governments that fail to fully integrate people with disabilities in programs and services violate this title.

2. Participation in Separate Programs. Under Title II, Subtitle A, state and local governments can offer programs that are specifically designed for people with disabilities; however, people cannot be forced to participate in such programs and cannot be denied the opportunity to participate in programs or activities that are not separate or different.

3. Right to Refuse an Accommodation. A person with a disability does not have to accept an accommodation if he or she so chooses. For example, an individual who is blind may choose not to avail himself or herself of the right to go to the front of a line, even if this privilege is made available.

4. Accommodation to the Regular Program. If a person with a disability decides not to participate in a special program, the state or local government is obligated to provide accommodations for that individual to benefit from the regular program. An example of this action includes a museum that provides a tour in sign language; however, if the deaf person so chooses, he or she can take the regular tour and accommodations will probably be required of the museum during the regular tour for that person.

5. Eligibility Criteria That Screen Out People With Disabilities. It is discrimination for a state or local government to apply eligibility criteria or standards that screen out or tend to screen out an individual with a disability. The wishes, tastes, or preferences of other clients or participants in programs may not be used to justify criteria that exclude or segregate people with disabilities.

6. Modifications in Policies. Reasonable modifications in policies and practices, and procedures when such modifications are nec-

essary to avoid discrimination on the basis of disability, are required under Title II. If a modification would alter the fundamental nature of a service, program, or activity, it is not required.

7. Association. It is discrimination under Title II for a state or local government to exclude or deny equal services, programs, or activities to an individual or entity because of the known disability of another individual with whom the individual or "entity" has a relationship or association. The term "entity" is included because, at times, organizations that provide services to, or are otherwise associated with, persons with disabilities are subjected to discrimination. The relationship does not necessarily need to be a family relationship; other kinds of relationships qualify for protection. An example of this form of discrimination might be a social service agency that refuses to provide services to a person because he or she lives with someone who has AIDS.

8. Charges. A state or local government cannot impose a surcharge on an individual with a disability or a group of individuals with disabilities to cover the cost of measures taken to comply with the ADA, such as the provision of auxiliary aids or program access.

9. Granting of Licenses and Certifications. Under Title II, a state or local government cannot discriminate against a qualified individual with a disability on the basis of the disability in granting licenses and certifications. A state or local government may not administer a licensing or certification program in a manner that subjects qualified individuals with disabilities to discrimination on the basis of disability, nor may a state or local government establish requirements for the programs or activities of licensing or certification that have the effect of limiting opportunities for participation or employment of people with disabilities. This means, in terms of social work licensing or certification laws, that a qualified individual with a disability who applies for a license or certification cannot be discriminated against on the basis of his or her disability during the application process.

10. Protection Against Retaliation. Under Title II, persons who file complaints are protected from retaliation and harassment by state or local government.

Not all requirements for Subtitle A are covered above. The ones listed do, however, provide an introduction to the basic requirements of this subtitle. Subtitle B is not discussed in this section; this aspect of the ADA covers public transportation.

Example Case Under Title II

In *L.C. v. Olmstead* (1997), Georgia state mental health officials were found to have violated Title II by continuing to institutionalize two mentally retarded individuals in a state mental hospital instead of providing them with community-based services. The claimants also suffered from emotional disabilities.

In this case, the U.S. District Court for the Northern District of Georgia ordered the state to provide the two claimants with appropriate community services. The court held that even though professional health care providers felt that the most appropriate place for the individuals was in community residential treatment, they continued to be confined to an institutional setting. The state of Georgia argued that they were denied community-based residential services because the state did not have resources to pay for the services. The court ruled that unnecessary institutional segregation of people with disabilities constitutes discrimination and the law clearly prohibits unnecessary institutionalization. Under Title II, public entities are required to make reasonable policy modifications to avoid disability discrimination unless such changes would fundamentally alter the nature of the program at issue. *L.C. v. Olmstead* clearly has tremendous implications for human services delivery and the profession of social work.

DISCRIMINATION ON THE BASIS OF DISABILITY

Harrison and Gilbert (1992) report findings from various testimonies made by individuals and representatives of various organizations concerning the need for the passage of the ADA. For example, Timothy Cook of the National Disability Action Center testified (Harrison and Gilbert, 1992:10):

As Rosa Parks taught us, and as the Supreme Court ruled thirty-five years ago in *Brown v. Board of Education*, segregation "affects one's heart and mind in ways that may never be undone. Separate but equal is inherently unequal."

Others testified that discrimination also included exclusion, or denial of benefits, services, or other opportunities that are as effective and meaningful as those provided to others. Furthermore, discrimination results from actions or inactions that discriminate by effect as well as by intention. Under these circumstances, discrimination includes the lack of access to buildings, standards and criteria, and practices based on thoughtlessness or indifference that discriminate against persons with disabilities (Harrison and Gilbert, 1992).

Testimony presented by Judith Heumann of the World Institute on Disability illustrated several forms of discrimination well known to people with disabilities. Heumann stated (Harrison and Gilbert, 1992:11):

When I was 5 my mother proudly pushed my wheelchair to our local public school, where I was promptly refused admission because the principal ruled that I was a fire hazard. I was forced to go into home instruction, receiving one hour of education twice a week for 3½ years. My entrance into mainstream society was blocked by discrimination and segregation. Segregation was not only on an institutional level but also acted as an obstruction to social integration. As a teenager, I could not travel with friends on the bus because it was not accessible. At my graduation from high school, the principal attempted to prevent me from accepting an award in a ceremony on stage simply because I was in a wheelchair.

Others echoing Heumann's experiences reported that having a history of a disability, being regarded as having a disability, or even associating with people with disabilities often resulted in discrimination. Discrimination also included the effects of a person's disability on others. For example, a child with Down's syndrome was refused admittance to a zoo because the zoo keeper felt the child would upset the chimpanzees. In another case a child with cerebral palsy was denied admission to school because the teacher claimed his physical appearance produced a nauseating effect on his classmates. During Senate testimony, Sen. Walter Mondale, a Minnesota Democrat, described a case in which a woman crippled by arthritis was denied a job not because she could not do the work, but because college trustees felt normal students should not see her. Finally, a number of individuals testified that they were denied jobs because they had AIDS, were former cancer victims, had epilepsy, or other serious illnesses (Harrison and Gilbert, 1992).

Major public opinion polls such as the Harris Poll found that by almost any definition, people with disabilities are uniquely underprivileged and disadvantaged. They are much poorer, much less educated, and have less social life and lower levels of self-satisfaction than other Americans (Harrison and Gilbert, 1992).

All of the data and testimony gathered by Congress that resulted in the passage of the ADA found that persons with disabilities experience discrimination in virtually every aspect of American life. They experience staggering levels of unemployment and poverty. Two-thirds of all people with disabilities between the ages of sixteen and sixty-four are not working, yet a large majority of those not working want to work. Sixty-six percent of unemployed working-aged people with disabilities wanted a job. What emerged from the research conducted by Congress was that persons with disabilities constituted one of the most oppressed minority groups in the United States (Harrison and Gilbert, 1992).

IMPLICATIONS OF THE ADA

The ADA is clearly grounded in the human rights philosophy. The act, like other civil rights legislation of the past, is aimed at an oppressed group, people with disabilities who have been denied equal opportunity to participate in the larger society.

It is significant that under the ADA, people with disabilities are defined as a minority group. This definition suggests that, for example, when a person with a disability is poor, it is less a result of a personal inadequacy than of a discriminatory society. Consequently, adjustment to a disability is not merely a personal problem, but one requiring the adjustment of the larger society to the person with a disability. This position requires that society adjust its attitudes and remove the obstacles it has placed in the way of self-fulfillment for persons with disabilities, including transportation and architecture systems designed only for the able, as well as the stereotypes that impugn the competence of people with disabilities.

The research suggests that, like other oppressed groups, people with disabilities have suffered tremendous discrimination. The National Council on Disability, the Civil Rights Commission, and recent national polls all concluded that discrimination against individuals with disabilities is pervasive in American society (*Governmental Affairs Newsletter*, 1991). This discrimination is sometimes a result of prejudice or patronizing attitudes; at other times it is the result of thoughtlessness or indifference. Whatever the origin, the outcomes are the same: segregation, exclusion, and the denial of equal, effective, and meaningful opportunities to participate in programs and activities. The ADA is aimed at preventing and correcting the numerous problems associated with discrimination against people with disabilities.

Another implication of the ADA is its focus on the philosophy of empowerment. The ADA is designed to help people take charge of their lives so they can partake of the great bounty this nation has to offer. As recent research (*Governmental Affairs Newsletter*, 1991) has found, "not working" is perhaps the truest definition of what it means to be a person with a disability in America. Ending discrimination against people with disabilities will have the direct impact of reducing the federal government's expenditure of $57 billion annually on disability benefits and programs that are premised on the dependency of individuals with disabilities. The ADA also has the effect of making people with disabilities into consumers and taxpayers. Furthermore, "when individuals move from being recipients of various types of welfare payments to skilled taxpaying workers, there are obviously many benefits not only for the individuals but for the whole society" (*Federal Register*, 1980:45). In essence, the ADA will help stop the discrimination against people with disabilities in the workplace— clearly, an outcome that will help empower this group through employment.

It is important to note that among the groups protected under the ADA are people who have AIDS. It is significant that employers cannot discriminate against a person with AIDS. The ADA thus provides critical protection to such people in the workplace.

In the final analysis, the most important implication of the ADA may well be that American society is finally changing its views on disabilities. No longer will people with disabilities be seen as individuals who must be hidden from public view through placement in institutions or simply as people who should be grateful for the disability programs currently in place. The ADA is having a positive impact on correcting the discrimination and segregation that people with disabilities have endured in the past. The ADA means that the individual with a disability has the same constitutional rights and privileges as the able person. As with other minority classifications, such as those based on race or sex, persons with disabilities are extended protections under the ADA that help them realize their full constitutional and human rights.

REFERENCES

Brothwell, D. S., and Sandison, A. T. (1967). *Diseases in antiquity.* Springfield, IL: Charles C. Thomas.

Burgdorf, R. L., and Burgdorf, M. P. (1977). The wicked witch is almost dead: *Buck v. Bell* and the sterilization of handicapped persons. *Temple Law Quarterly* 50: 995–1054.

EEOC v. AIC Security Investigations LTD. (1993). *BNA'S Americans With Disabilities Act manual (1995).* Washington, DC: Bureau of National Affairs.

Equal Employment Opportunity Commission and U.S. Department of Justice. (1992). *The Americans With Disabilities Act: Questions and answers.* Washington, DC: National Institute on Disabilities and Rehabilitation Research.

Federal Register. (1980). No. 66. Washington, DC: U.S. Government Printing Office.

Fiedler, L. (1978). *Freaks.* New York: Simon and Schuster.

Galdston, I. (Ed.) (1963). *Man's image in medicine and anthropology.* New York: International Universities Press.

Gellman, W. (1959). Roots of prejudice against the handicapped. *Journal of Rehabilitation* 25: 4–6.

Government Affairs Newsletter (1991). Vol. 25, No. 10. Columbia, MO: University of Missouri.

Great Plains Disability and Business Technical Assistance Center (1995). *Americans With Disabilities Act technical assistance manual Title II.* Columbia, MO: Great Plains Disability and Business Technical Assistance Center.

Harrison, M., and Gilbert, S. (Eds.) (1992). *The Americans With Disabilities Act handbook.* Beverly Hills, CA: Excellent Books.

Hull, K. (1977). The specter of equality: Reflections on civil rights of physically handicapped persons. *Temple Law Quarterly* 50: 944–952.

Ianacone, B. P. (1977). Historical overview: From charity to rights. *Temple Law Quarterly* 50: 953–960.

L. C. v. Olmstead. (1997). *BNA'S Americans With Disabilities Act manual (1997).* Washington, DC: Bureau of National Affairs.

Newman, J. (1987). Background forces in policies for care and treatment of disability. *Marriage and Family Review* 11: 25–44.

Pardeck, J. T., and Chung, W. S. (1992). An analysis of the Americans With Disabilities Act of 1990. *Journal of Health and Social Policy* 4: 47–56.

Spencer, M. P. (1995). The Americans With Disabilities Act: Description and analysis. In J. G. Veres and R. R. Sims, eds. *Human resource management and the Americans With Disabilities Act* (pp. 7–39). Westport, CT: Quorum Books.

Sussman, M. B. (Ed.) (1965). *Sociology and rehabilitation.* Washington, DC: American Sociological Association.

Chapter 2

An Overview of the Technical Aspects of Title I

Professional social workers, regardless of practice setting, should be aware of the technical aspects of Title I of the ADA. As covered in Chapter 1, Title I deals with the employment requirements of the ADA. Title I prohibits discrimination against people with disabilities by private employers, state and local governments, employment agencies, labor organizations, and labor-management committees. All employers with fifteen or more employees, including state and local government employers, are covered by the employment provisions of Title I. The Equal Employment Opportunity Commission (EEOC) enforces Title I. Disability discrimination is investigated through the same procedures used to investigate racial and other kinds of discrimination. What this means to social work agencies is that employment discrimination based on disability should be treated as seriously as other forms of discrimination in the workplace.

The EEOC investigates and attempts to resolve charges of discrimination by employees. Title I makes it unlawful to discriminate in any aspect of employment, including recruitment, hiring, promotion, training, layoffs, pay, firing, job assignments, leave, and benefits. It is critical to stress to co-workers or supervisors that retaliation against an employee who files a complaint with the EEOC is also a violation of the ADA. An employee who feels he or she has been discriminated against on the basis of disability must file a complaint within 180 days of the act of discrimination, unless there is a state or local law that also provides relief for discrimination on the basis of disability. In most cases where there is such a law, the complainant has 300 days to file a charge (Equal Employment Opportunity Commission and U.S. Department of Justice, 1992).

The EEOC publishes educational materials and provides training for employers. The EEOC's technical assistance program is separate and distinct from its enforcement responsibilities. If an employer seeks information or assistance from the EEOC, the employer will not be subject to any enforcement action because of such inquiries. The EEOC also recognizes that differences and disputes about Title I will arise between employers and people with disabilities as a result of misunderstanding. Such disputes often can be resolved more effectively through informal negotiation or mediation procedures than through the formal enforcement process of the ADA. The EEOC attempts to encourage this form of dispute resolution if it does not deprive any individual of legal rights provided under Title I (Equal Employment Opportunity Commission and U.S. Department of Justice, 1992).

QUESTIONS AND ANSWERS ON TITLE I

The following questions and answers will help professional social workers better understand the technical aspects of Title I. The information is based on materials published by the EEOC (Equal Employment Opportunity Commission and U.S. Department of Justice, 1992).

Question: What is the relationship between the ADA and the Rehabilitation Act of 1973?

Answer: The Rehabilitation Act of 1973 prohibits discrimination on the basis of handicap by the federal government, federal contractors, and recipients of federal financial assistance. If a social work agency, for example, is covered by the Rehabilitation Act prior to the passage of the ADA, the ADA will not affect coverage. Many of the provisions contained in the ADA are based on Section 504 of the Rehabilitation Act and its implementing regulations. If a social work agency receives federal financial assistance and is in compliance with Section 504, it probably is in compliance with the ADA requirements affecting employment except in those areas where the ADA contains additional requirements. If an employer receives federal assistance, the non-discrimination requirements under Section 503 of the Rehabilitation Act will essentially be the same as those under Title I; however, an employer will continue to have additional affirmative action requirements under Section 503 that do not exist under Title I.

Question: If a social work agency has several qualified applicants for a position, does Title I require the agency to hire the applicant with a disability?

Answer: No. The social work agency, like any employer, can hire the most qualified applicant. Title I only makes it unlawful for an employer to discriminate against a qualified individual with a disability on the basis of disability.

Question: Under Title I, who is a "qualified individual with a disability"?

Answer: A qualified individual with a disability is a person who meets legitimate skill, experience, educational, or other requirements of an employment position that he or she holds or seeks, and who can perform the "essential functions" of the position with or without reasonable accommodation. Requiring the ability to perform "essential functions" ensures that an individual with a disability will not be considered unqualified simply because of inability to perform marginal or incidental job functions. If the individual is qualified to perform essential job functions except for limitations caused by a disability, the employer must consider whether the individual could perform these functions with a reasonable accommodation. If a written job description has been prepared for advertising or interviewing applicants for a job, this will be considered as evidence, although not conclusive evidence, of the essential functions of the job.

Question: If an employee of a social work agency is diabetic and takes insulin to control his or her diabetes, is the employee protected by Title I of the ADA?

Answer: Yes, the determination as to whether a person has a disability under Title I is made without regard to mitigating measures such as medications, auxiliary aids, and reasonable accommodations. If an employee has an impairment that substantially limits a major life activity, he or she is protected under Title I, regardless of whether the disease or condition or its effects may be corrected or controlled.

Question: An employee in a social work agency breaks his arm and is temporarily unable to perform the essential functions of his job as a typist. Is the employee protected by Title I?

Answer: No, even though this employee has an impairment, it does not substantially limit a major life activity if it is of limited duration and will have no long-term effect.

Question: Is a social work agency obligated to provide a reasonable accommodation for an individual if the agency is unaware of the employee's disability?

Answer: No, an employer's obligation to provide reasonable accommodation applies only to known physical or mental impairments of employees. However, this does not mean that an applicant, for example, must always inform an agency of a disability. If a disability is obvious—if, for example, the applicant uses a wheelchair—the social work agency knows of the disability even if the applicant never mentions it.

Question: How can a social work agency determine whether a reasonable accommodation is appropriate and the type of accommodation that should be made available?

Answer: The requirement generally will be triggered by a request from an individual with a disability, who frequently can recommend an appropriate accommodation. Accommodations must be made on a case-by-case basis, because the nature and extent of a disabling condition and the requirements of the job will vary. The core test in selecting a particular type of accommodation is that of effectiveness, that is, whether the accommodation will enable the individual with a disability to perform the essential functions of the job. The accommodation does not have to be the best, or the one the person with a disability prefers, although primary consideration should be given to the preference of the individual involved. A social work agency, like any employer, has the discretion to choose between effective accommodations, and may select one that is least expensive or easiest to provide.

Question: Can a social work agency consider reassigning an employee with a disability to another position as a reasonable accommodation?

Answer: When an employee with a disability is unable to perform a job even with the provision of a reasonable accommodation, an agency must consider reassigning the employee to an existing position that he or she can perform with or without a reasonable accommodation. This requirement applies only to employees and not to applicants for jobs within the agency. An agency is not required to create a position or bump another employee to create a vacancy; neither does an agency have to promote an employee with a disability to a higher-level position.

Question: What if an applicant or employee refuses to accept an accommodation that a social work agency offers?

Answer: Title I stipulates that an employer cannot require a qualified individual with a disability to accept an accommodation that is neither requested nor needed by the individual. However, if a necessary reasonable accommodation is refused, the individual may be considered not qualified.

Question: A social work agency has a consulting firm develop a training course for its employees; the firm arranges for the course to be held at a hotel that is inaccessible to one of its employees. Is the agency liable under Title I?

Answer: Yes, an employer may not do through a contractual or other relationship what it is prohibited from doing directly. Under Title I, the employer is required to provide a location that is readily accessible to and usable by employees with disabilities unless such a situation would create an undue hardship.

Question: Does a social work agency as an employer have to ensure that the agency is accessible?

Answer: Under Title I, an employer is responsible for making facilities accessible to qualified applicants and employees with disabilities as a reasonable accommodation, unless this would cause an undue hardship. Accessibility must be provided to enable an applicant to participate in the application process, to enable a qualified person with a disability to perform esoteric job functions, and to enable him or her to have access to benefits and privileges available to other employees.

Question: Under Title I, can a social work agency refuse to hire an individual or fire a current employee who uses drugs illegally?

Answer: Yes, persons who use illegal drugs are not protected by Title I. However, Title I does not exclude persons from protection if they have successfully completed or are currently in a rehabilitation program and are no longer using illegal drugs. Persons who are erroneously regarded as engaging in illegal drug usage are also protected by Title I.

Question: Does Title I protect people with AIDS?

Answer: Yes, Title I protects people with AIDS, or those who have tested HIV-positive, from discrimination.

Question: Can a social work agency consider health and safety in deciding whether to hire an applicant or retain an employee with a disability?

Answer: Title I permits an employer to require that an individual not pose a direct threat to the health and safety of the individual or others in the workplace. A direct threat means a significant risk of substantial harm. A social work agency cannot fire or refuse to hire an individual because of a slightly increased risk of harm to him or her or others. Neither can an agency do so based on a speculative or remote risk. The determination that an individual poses a direct threat must be based on objective, factual evidence regarding the individual's current ability to perform essential functions of a job. If an applicant or employee with a disability poses a direct threat to the health or safety of himself or others, the agency must consider whether the risk can be eliminated or reduced to acceptable levels with a reasonable accommodation.

Question: Is a social work agency required to provide additional insurance for employees with disabilities?

Answer: No, Title I requires only that an employer provide an employee with a disability equal access to whatever health insurance coverage other employees have. As an example, if an agency's health insurance coverage for certain treatments is limited to a specific number per year, and an employee because of his or her disability needs more than the specified number, Title I does not require the agency to provide additional coverage to meet that employee's health insurance needs.

Question: Does the ADA require a social work agency to post a notice explaining the act's requirements?

Answer: The ADA requires that employers post a notice in an accessible form to applicants and employees describing the provisions of the act. The EEOC will provide the employer with posters summarizing the nondiscrimination requirements of the ADA.

TITLE I AND PSYCHIATRIC DISABILITIES

The modern workforce includes many people with psychiatric disabilities who often face discrimination because of their disability. Title I attempts to combat employment discrimination against people with psychiatric disabilities. The following discussion is based on recent regulations released by the EEOC (Equal Employment Opportunity Commission, 1997). It is particularly relevant to social work agencies given the profession's longstanding commitment to meeting the needs of oppressed people. Professional social workers should use the following information also as a general guide to understanding the legal requirements of Title I for all disabilities protected by the ADA.

One of the leading areas in which people file complaints of alleged discrimination is that of psychiatric disabilities. As can be seen in Table I, it is the second most common reason for filing charges of discrimination with the EEOC. These charges were based on psychiatric disabilities such as anxiety disorders, depression, bipolar disorder, schizophrenia, and other psychiatric impairments.

Psychiatric Disability Under Title I

As covered in Chapter 1, under the ADA the term disability means: (1) A physical or mental impairment that substantially limits one or more of the major life activities of an individual; (2) a record of such an impairment; and (3) being regarded as having such an impairment. The following will focus on the first prong of the ADA's definition of a disability.

The ADA defines a mental impairment to include any mental or psychological disorder, such as emotional or mental illness. Examples of emotional or mental illnesses include major depression, bipolar disorder, anxiety disorders, schizophrenia, and personality disorders. The current edition of the American Psychiatric Association's *Diagnostic and Statistical Manual of Mental Disorders* (American Psychiatric Association, 1994) is relevant for identifying these disabilities. The *DSM-IV* is recognized as an important reference by the courts and is widely used by mental health professionals for diagnoses.

It is noted, however, that not all conditions listed in the *DSM-IV* are disabilities under the ADA. For example, the *DSM-IV* lists conditions that are excluded from ADA coverage such as a person who uses illegal drugs or a person who abuses his or her spouse or children. These kinds of conditions are clearly disorders in the *DSM-IV*; however, they are not impairments under the ADA. Furthermore, traits or behaviors in and of themselves are not mental impairments. For example, stress in itself is not a mental impairment. However, if stress can be shown to be related to a mental or physical impairment, it would be considered a disability. Similarly, traits like irritability, chronic lateness, and poor judgment are not in themselves mental impairments, although they may well be linked to an impairment.

Major Life Activities

A mental impairment must substantially limit one or more major life activities to be considered a disability under Title I. Major life activities limited by a mental impairment differ from person to person. There is no exhaustive list of major life activities; however, mental impairments often restrict major life activities such as learning, thinking, concentrating, interacting with others, caring for oneself, speaking, performing manual tasks, or working. Sleeping is also considered a major life activity that may be limited by mental impairments.

Substantial Limitation

Substantial limitation is assessed in terms of the severity of the limitation and the length of time it restricts a major life activity.

The determination that an individual has a substantially limiting impairment should be based on information about how the impairment affects that person and not on generalizations about the condition. When deciding if an impairment substantially limits one's functioning, this analysis should include the individual's typical functioning at home, at work, and in other settings; it must also be established that the individual's functional limitations are linked to his or her mental impairment. What is important is the fact that expert testimony about substantial limitation is not necessarily required. In fact, credible testimony from the individual with a mental impairment and his or her family members, friends, or co-workers may suffice.

An emotional impairment substantially limits a major life activity if it prevents a person from performing a major life function or significantly restricts the condition, manner, or duration under which an individual can perform a major life activity, as compared with the typical person in the general population. A mental impairment does not significantly restrict a major life activity if it results in only mild limitations.

When considering whether a mental impairment is corrected by medication, it should be recognized that the impairment continues to substantially limit major life activities even though the severity of the impairment has been reduced. The ADA unequivocally concludes that the extent to which an impairment limits performance of a major life activity is assessed without regard to mitigating measures, including medications. Consequently, an individual who is taking medication for a mental impairment has a disability under Title I if there is evidence that the impairment, when left untreated, substantially limits a major life activity.

Generally, an emotional impairment is substantially limiting if it lasts for more than several months and significantly restricts the performance of one or more major life activities during a given period. It is not substantially limiting if it lasts for only a brief time or does not significantly restrict an individual's ability to perform a major life activity. Whether the impairment is substantially limiting is assessed without regard to mitigating measures such as medication. An example of this kind of situation is as follows:

> An employee of a social work agency has had major depression for almost a year. She has been intensely sad and socially withdrawn, except for going to work. The person has also suffered from serious insomnia and has had severe problems concentrating. This employee has an impairment, major depression, that significantly restricts her ability to interact with others, to sleep, and to concentrate. The effects of this impairment are severe and have lasted long enough to substantially limit major life activities.

In addition, some mental impairments may be long term, or potentially long term, in that their duration is indefinite and unknowable or is expected to be at least several months. These kinds of conditions, if severe enough, may constitute a disability. However, conditions that are temporary and have no permanent or long-term effects on an individual's major life activities are not substantially limiting. An example might be a person who has broken his or her arm. The effects of this kind of condition are short term.

Chronic, episodic conditions may constitute substantially limiting impairments if they are substantially limiting when active or have a high likelihood of recurrence in substantially limiting forms. Psychiatric impairments such as bipolar disorder, major depression, and schizophrenia may remit and intensify, sometimes repeatedly, over the course of months or years.

Finally, a mental impairment substantially limits an employee's ability to interact with others if, due to the impairment, he or she is significantly restricted as compared with the typical person in the general population. Unfriendliness with co-workers or a supervisor would not, standing alone, be sufficient to establish a substantial limitation in interacting with others. An employee would be substantially limited, however, if his or her relations with others were characterized on a regular basis by severe problems such as consistently high levels of hostility, social withdrawal, or failure to communicate when necessary. These kinds of conditions must be long term or potentially long term to be considered a disability under Title I. The following example illustrates when a mental impairment becomes a disability:

> An employee of a social work agency who is diagnosed with schizophrenia works successfully as a computer programmer in the agency. Before finding an effective medication, she stayed in her room at home for several months, usually refusing to talk to family and close friends. After finding an effective medication, she was able to return to school, graduate, and begin working in the agency. This individual has a mental impairment, schizophrenia, that substantially limits her ability to interact with others when evaluated without medication.

Under Title I, this employee has a disability. Professional social workers should also note that not only emotional disabilities are protected under the employment provisions of the ADA. Other related limitations can be substantial limitations. These include learning disabilities, neurological disorders, and physical trauma to the brain (e.g., stroke, brain tumor, or head injuries).

Disclosure of an Emotional Impairment

Individuals with psychiatric disabilities often have questions about whether and when they should disclose an emotional impairment. A major concern for this protected group is whether the disclosure will have negative consequences for them in the workplace. Once this information is revealed by a job applicant or an employee, it has tremendous implications under Title I of the ADA.

An employer cannot ask questions that are likely to elicit information about a person's emotional disability before making a job offer. Questions on a job application about psychiatric disability or mental or emotional illness or about treatment are likely to elicit information about a psychiatric disability and therefore are prohibited before an employment offer is made. Later in this chapter, a list of appropriate and inappropriate questions is presented.

An employer may only ask questions related to a psychiatric impairment or about a disability in limited circumstances. The ADA is clear on the point that this cannot occur before employment except when an applicant requests a reasonable accommodation for the hiring process. If the need for an accommodation is not obvious, an employer may ask an applicant for reasonable documentation about his or her disability. The employer may require the applicant to provide documentation from an appropriate professional concerning his or her disability and functional limitations. A variety of professionals, including social workers, can provide this documentation.

An employer would make it clear to the applicant that he or she is requesting such information simply to verify the existence of a disability and the need for an accommodation. Information may be requested by the prospective employer only to accomplish these limited purposes. The following is an example of how this process works:

> An applicant for a position in a social work agency asks to take a typing test in a quiet location rather than in a busy reception area because of his medical condition. The agency may make disability-related inquiries at this point because the applicant's need for reasonable accommodation under the ADA is not obvious based on the statement that an accommodation is needed because of a medical condition. Specifically, the agency may ask the applicant to provide documentation showing that he has an impairment that substantially limits a major life activity and that he needs to take the typing test in a quiet location because of disability-related functional limitations.

Even though an employer cannot ask an applicant if he or she will need a reasonable accommodation for a job, an exception can be made if the employer believes, before making a job offer, that the applicant will need accommodation to perform the functions of the job. For a person with a non-visible disability, this may occur if the individual voluntarily discloses his or her disability or if the person voluntarily tells the employer that he or she needs reasonable accommodation to perform the job. The employer then may ask the following limited questions:

1. Does the applicant need reasonable accommodations?

2. What type of reasonable accommodation would be needed to perform the functions of the job?

The only clear circumstance in which an employer can legally ask questions related to an applicant's disability, including an emotional disability, is after an offer of employment. After an employer extends an offer of employment, the employer may require a medical examination, including questions about psychiatric disability, if the employer subjects all employees in the same job category to the same inquiries or examinations regardless of disability.

When an employer has been informed of an applicant's or employee's psychiatric disability, this information becomes confidential under the ADA. This information must be stored separately from the usual personnel files. The only individuals within an organization that legally can have information on the individual's psychiatric disability are the following (Great Plains Disability and Business Technical Assistance Center, 1995):

1. A supervisor may need the information to ensure the appropriate accommodations for the employee are provided.

2. First aid and safety personnel may be told if the disability might require emergency treatment.

3. Government officials investigating compliance with the ADA must be given relevant information concerning an employee's disability on request.

Finally, if other employees ask questions about a co-worker's disability, the employer may not disclose any medical information in response. An employer may not tell other employees whether he or she is providing a reasonable accommodation for a particular individual. Given this kind of situation, it is particularly important for social work agencies, or any employer, to have training on the ADA, including the obligation to provide reasonable accommodations.

Requesting Reasonable Accommodation

Employers must provide a reasonable accommodation to the physical or mental limitations of a qualified person with a disability unless they can show that the accommodation would impose an undue hardship for the organization.

Employees with disabilities at times are reluctant to request reasonable accommodations because of the potential negative consequences.

A person who requests a reasonable accommodation for a psychiatric disability should follow a procedure. The individual or his or her representative must let the employer know that he or she needs an adjustment or change at work for reasons related to a medical condition. The following is an example of how the process works:

> An employee of a social work agency requests time off because she is depressed and stressed. This request can simply be written in "plain English" and does not have to be in a highly technical form. This kind of statement is sufficient to put the employer on notice that the employee is requesting a reasonable accommodation. However, if the employee's need for accommodation is not obvious, the agency may ask for reasonable documentation concerning the employee's disability and functional limitations.

It is also noted that someone other than the employee with a disability can request a reasonable accommodation for the employee, including family members, friends, health professionals, or others who may be familiar with the person. The employee, according to the ADA, can refuse to take an accommodation if it is not needed.

Requests for reasonable accommodations do not have to be in writing. An employee can request an accommodation at any time during employment. The employer can require the employee to go to a health care professional of the employer's choice for purposes of documenting the need for reasonable accommodation and disability.

Reasonable accommodations for persons with disabilities must be determined on a case-by-case basis because workplaces and jobs vary, as do people with disabilities. Accommodations for people with psychiatric disabilities may involve changes to workplace polices, procedures, or practice. Physical changes in the workplace or extra equipment also may be effective reasonable accommodations for some individuals.

In some instances, the precise nature of an effective accommodation for an individual with a psychiatric disability may not be apparent. Thus, mental health professionals may have to help employers and employees to communicate effectively about reasonable accommodation. The following briefly covers types of reasonable accommodation that may be effective for certain individuals with psychiatric disabilities.

One kind of reasonable accommodation might be to provide the employee with time off from work or a modified work schedule. For example, the employee might change the work schedule to 10 A.M. to 6 P.M. rather than 9 A.M. to 5 P.M. Some medications taken for psychiatric disabilities cause extreme grogginess and prevent the individual from concentrating early in the morning. Depending on the job, a later work schedule may enable the employee to perform essential job functions.

Physical changes in the workplace or equipment can serve as accommodations for people with psychiatric disabilities. For example, room dividers, partitions, or other soundproofing or visual barriers between work spaces may accommodate individuals who have disability-related limitations in concentration. Moving an individual away from noisy office machinery or reducing workplace noise can be a reasonable accommodation. Permitting an employee to wear headphones to block out noise can also be an effective accommodation.

A reasonable accommodation may be modifying workplace policy. For example, a social work agency may provide a reasonable accommodation that allows a person with a disability who has problems concentrating to take detailed notes during an interview with a client. Even though this practice may be discouraged for other social workers by agency policy, it may be a reasonable accommodation for a person with a disability related to concentration.

A final example of a reasonable accommodation for a person with a psychiatric disability might be adjusting supervisory methods. The following provides an example of this kind of adjustment:

> An employee of a social work agency requests more daily guidance and feedback as a reasonable accommodation for limitations associated with a psychiatric disability. In response to her request, the employer consults with the employee, her health care professional, and her supervisor about how her limitations are manifested in the office. For example, the employee is unable to stay focused on the steps necessary to complete large projects. As a result of consultations, the supervisor and employee work out a long-term plan to initiate weekly meetings to review the status of large projects and to identify which steps need to be taken.

One final point on reasonable accommodation is that employers have no legal obligation to ensure that a person with a psychiatric disability takes his or her medication.

ADA CHECKLIST

The goal of this chapter is to provide detail about the technical aspects of Title I. The following checklist provides the professional social worker with information on the kinds of activities that are allowed under the ADA. A yes or no follows each statement; those statements that are answered with a no should alert the agency to modify an employment practice.

Recruitment Practices

1. All positions (not just entry level) are open to qualified applicants with disabilities.
   Yes ——— No ———

2. Job openings are posted in accessible formats.
   Yes ——— No ———

3. Interview areas are readily accessible without barriers.
   Yes ——— No ———

4. The testing administered does not discriminate against applicants with sensory or speaking impairments.
   Yes ——— No ———

5. All tests and selection criteria for a position are related to the position and consistent with business necessity.
   Yes ——— No ———

6. Selection criteria directly relate to the job description.
   Yes ——— No ———

7. Applicants are not asked if they have a disability, or the nature or extent of any disability. (An employer may ask about their ability to perform specific essential job functions.)
   Yes ——— No ———

8. Relationships with individuals with disabilities are not used as a reason for non-selection.
   Yes ——— No ———

9. Safety-related concerns are specific only to essential job functions.
   Yes ——— No ———

10. No pre-employment medical examinations are required as part of the selection process unless they are required of all new employees.
    Yes ———   No ———

11. Medical information is retained on separate forms and in separate medical files.
    Yes ———   No ———

12. Medical history and information are treated confidentially.
    Yes ———   No ———

13. Medical information is shared confidentially with managers and supervisors if it deals with activity restrictions.
    Yes ———   No ———

14. Medical information is shared confidentially with first aid and emergency treatment personnel.
    Yes ———   No ———

15. Medical information is shared with government personnel investigating ADA compliance.
    Yes ———   No ———

Employment

16. Reasonable accommodations are made in initial and subsequent positions, unless they impose an undue business hardship.
    Yes ———   No ———

17. Facilities used by all employees are accessible and easily usable by individuals with disabilities.
    Yes ———   No ———

18. When necessary, jobs are redesigned to eliminate minor tasks.
    Yes ———   No ———

19. When necessary, tasks are reassigned to other positions.
    Yes ———   No ———

20. Adaptive aids and Assistive Technology applications are used when they do not impose undue financial hardships.
    Yes ———   No ———

21. Part-time and modified work schedules are considered reasonable accommodations.
    Yes ———   No ———

22. Transfer to open positions for which an employee with a disability is qualified is considered.
   Yes _____   No _____

23. Readers, interpreters, and attendants are provided when not an undue hardship.
   Yes _____   No _____

24. Applicants and employees are informed of an employer's obligations under the ADA.
   Yes _____   No _____

25. Notice of rights under the ADA is posted in an accessible format in a prominent place.
   Yes _____   No _____

INTERVIEWING GUIDELINES

As a result of the ADA, certain questions about an individual's disability or health condition are not permissible. The use of questions during the interview process regarding disability or health may be construed as evidence of discrimination against an individual with a disability. It is extremely important that anyone involved in job selection be aware of and avoid the use of questions or language that may be interpreted as discriminatory. The following list provides examples of questions that an employer may and may not ask in an interview.

Don't: ask a candidate if he or she has any disabilities.

Don't: ask a candidate if he or she has ever had any disabilities or has ever been considered disabled.

Do: ask the candidate if he or she is able to perform the essential functions of the position.

Don't: ask a candidate if he or she has any medical or health problems.

Don't: ask a candidate if he or she has any physical or mental limitations.

Do: ask the candidate if he or she has a good safety record.

Don't: ask a candidate what degree or kind of limitations he or she may have for obvious or observable disabilities.

Do: ask candidates if there are any essential duties that they feel they could not perform.

Don't: ask candidates if their spouse, dependents, family members, or friends have any disabilities or health problems.

Don't: ask a candidate if he or she is or has been a member of any organization supporting disabilities programs.

Do: ask a candidate if he or she is willing to comply with the agency's policies on affirmative action, nondiscrimination, and sexual harassment.

Don't: ask a candidate if he or she has ever had any drug or alcohol abuse problems.

Do: ask the candidate if he or she would be willing to take a pre-employment drug test.

Don't: ask a candidate if he or she must take any prescribed medication regularly.

Don't: ask a candidate if he or she must take time off regularly to see a physician or have medical treatments.

Don't: ask a candidate what accommodations he or she would need to perform the job duties.

Do: ask a candidate what specific accommodations he or she would need, but only if the candidate raises the issue first.

Don't: ask a candidate if he or she would take a pre-employment medical examination prior to a job offer.

Don't: ask a candidate if he or she has ever been refused health or life insurance.

Don't: ask a candidate if he or she has ever received Workers Compensation or disability pay from another employer.

Don't: ask a candidate if he or she has ever been rejected from military service for medical reasons.

Do: Ask a candidate if he or she has had any on-the-job accidents involving personal or property damage.

The above are only a few of the many questions that may and may not be asked under the ADA. An excellent rule of thumb to use when interviewing candidates is, if in doubt about a question, do not ask it.

JOB DESCRIPTION

An important practice that social work agencies should follow is to develop job descriptions for every position in an agency. This description should include the primary purpose of the job, its essential functions, and qualifications. Even though the ADA does not require a job description, they are an important line of defense against a Title I complaint by a job applicant or employee. The following provides an example of a job description that contains elements critical to the ADA.

Job Description: Personnel Technician

Primary Purpose: Performs technical personnel work in any major function of the Personnel Department such as employment, wage and classification, or training as assigned.

Supervision: Under general supervision of assigned coordinator.

Description of Work

Essential Functions

1. Performs responsible activities in the areas of employment, classification, or training as required.

2. Screens applications for minimum qualifications, conducts interviews of applicants, and certifies names to appointing authorities.

3. Develops, revises, and administers a variety of writing and skills tests, including scoring the results and establishing eligibility lists.

4. Gathers, reviews, and analyzes data and makes recommendations for improved recruitment procedures.

5. Conducts reference, background, and employment checks on eligible candidates.

6. Performs classification studies on new and existing positions, completes job analysis, and makes recommendations.

7. Develops and revises job descriptions, including reviewing job analysis questionnaires to determine essential functions of a position.

8. Completes salary and benefit surveys, assists in conducting the agency's annual survey, and compiles results and prepares reports.

9. Assists in developing training programs, coordinating training activities, developing lesson plans, and serving as an instructor as assigned.

10. Helps determine and assess training needs, prepares recommendations, and develops or locates training aides and materials as assigned.

11. Assists the Equal Employment Opportunity (EEO) technician by providing necessary information to complete required EEO reports and affirmative-action plans.

12. Maintains records and prepares reports for assigned area.

13. Utilizes computer software applications such as word processing, spreadsheet, and database.

14. Rotates assignments through or assists any functional program of the Personnel Department as required.

Important Functions

1. Performs office administration tasks such as copying, faxing, and filing.

2. Assists with job fairs.

Qualifications Required

Knowledge. Principles and methods of at least one of the following: recruitment and selection techniques, classification and job analysis, compensation and salary administration, or training and development; personnel law such as Title VII, the Fair Labor Standards Act, the Americans With Disabilities Act; computer applications such as word processing, spreadsheet, and database.

Abilities. Conduct effective interviews, job audits, and training as assigned; perform independently and exercise sound judgment; prepare and present clear and concise reports; work effectively in a team environment that promotes Total Quality Management; read and understand a variety of information including applications, laws, agency policies; accurately enter data into and operate a computer; follow oral and written instructions; communicate effectively verbally and in writing; deal effectively and courteously with associates and clients; perform essential functions of the job without posing a direct threat to the health and safety of others.

Experience, Education, and Training. Graduation from a recognized college or university with a bachelor's degree in public, personnel or business administration or in a related field supplemented by at least one year of responsible experience in personnel work. Directly related experience may be substituted for the degree requirement on a year-for-year basis.

Physical Requirements. Perform bending, climbing, and reaching from ground level to six feet in height; may lift and carry up to fifty pounds and push and pull up to 180 pounds depending on assignment; be able to hold and grip objects; be able to observe and move with applicants and/or employees when conducting tests; possess the manual dexterity necessary to operate a computer keyboard.

Working Environment. Primarily indoors, with heating and cooling regulated in a general office environment.

Licensing/Certification. None

Miscellaneous Requirements. None

The above job description serves as an example of what should be developed for all positions in an agency. Even though it is not a requirement of the ADA to develop job descriptions, it is highly recommended. If an ADA complaint under Title I is filed against a social work agency, the job description is the agency's first line of defense against the complaint.

EEOC COMPLAINTS UNDER TITLE I

From July 26, 1992, through September 30, 1996, the 72,687 charges filed with the Equal Employment Opportunity Commission were largely allegations of discrimination based on hidden disabilities (see Table 2.1).

The top twelve disabilities cited by complainants included back impairments, mental illness, and cancer. Bennett-Alexander and Pincus (1995) suggest hidden disabilities will be the area in which most complaints will continue to be filed with the EEOC. One explanation for this phenomenon may be that employers are more cautious in their treatment of people with obvious disabilities than they are with people with hidden disabilities, thus resulting in a higher number of discrimination complaints filed by the latter group. Research is called for on this problem area.

Table 2.2 lists the ADA violations most often cited under Title I. It can be seen that discharge is the most common reason a charge of discrimination was filed, constituting over 50 percent of the cases. Failure to provide reasonable accommodation included over 28 percent of the charges. It is interesting to note that 12 percent of the charges were for harassment. Charges of discrimination can be resolved in the following ways:

Table 2.1
Disabilities Most Often Cited as the Basis of Discrimination Complaints
with the EEOC from July 26, 1992, Through September 30, 1996

Disabilities Cited	Percentage
Back impairments	18.2
Emotional/psychiatric impairments	12.7
Neurological impairments	11.3
Extremities	9.0
Heart impairments	4.1
Diabetes	3.6
Substance abuse	3.3
Hearing impairments	2.9
Vision impairments	2.6
Blood disorders HIV (subcategory of blood disorders)	2.4
Cancer	2.3
Asthma	1.7

Note: There were 72,687 total charges.(This is not a complete list; therefore, percentages do not add up to 100.)
Source: Equal Employment Opportunity Commission, October 1996. TADAR: The ADA Report (Vol. 6, No. 1), 1997, Columbia, MO: University of Missouri.

Administrative Closure

A charge closed for administrative reasons may include: failure to locate the charging party, the charging party failed to respond to EEOC communications, the charging party refused to accept full relief, the outcome of related litigation established a precedent that makes further processing of the charge futile, or the charging party requested withdrawal of a charge without receiving benefits or having resolved the issue.

Merit Resolution

These are charges with outcomes favorable to charging parties and/or charges with meritorious allegations. Included are negotiated settlements, withdrawal with benefits, successful conciliations, and unsuccessful conciliations.

Table 2.2
ADA Violations Most Often Cited as the Basis of Discrimination Complaints with the EEOC from July 26, 1992, Through September 30, 1996

Violations Cited	Percentage
Discharge	51.9
Failure to provide reasonable accommodation	28.1
Harassment	12.0
Hiring	9.8
Discipline	7.8
Layoff	4.7
Promotion	3.9
Benefits	3.9
Wages	3.4
Rehire	3.4
Suspension	2.2

Note: This list adds up to more than 100 percent because individuals can allege multiple violations. Percentages are rounded off.
Source: Equal Employment Opportunity Commission, October 1996. TADAR: The ADA Report (Vol. 6, No. 1), 1997, Columbia, MO: University of Missouri.

No Reasonable Cause

This is the EEOC's determination that there is reasonable cause to believe that discrimination occurred, based on evidence obtained in an investigation. The charging party may request a review of a no-cause finding by EEOC headquarters officials and may exercise the right to bring private court action.

Reasonable Cause

In a determination of reasonable cause, the EEOC believes that discrimination occurred based on evidence obtained in investigation. Reasonable-cause determinations are generally followed by efforts to conciliate the discriminatory issues that gave rise to the initial charge. Note that some reasonable-cause findings are resolved through negotiated settlements, withdrawals with benefits, and other types of resolution, which are not characterized as either successful or unsuccessful conciliations.

Settlements (Negotiated)

These are charges settled with benefits to the charging party as warranted by evidence of record. In such cases, the EEOC is a party to the settlement agreement between the charging party and the respondent (an employer, union, or other entity covered by EEOC-enforced statutes).

Successful Conciliation

A charge with reasonable-cause determination is closed after successful conciliation. Successful conciliation results in substantial relief to the charging party and all others adversely affected by the discrimination.

Unsuccessful Conciliation

A charge with reasonable-cause determination is closed after efforts to conciliate the charge are unsuccessful. Pursuant to EEOC policy, the charge will be closed and reviewed for litigation consideration.

Withdrawal With Benefits

A charge is withdrawn by the charging party on receipt of desired benefits. The withdrawal may take place after a settlement or after the respondent grants the appropriate benefit to the charging party.

Of the 72,687 charges filed between July 26, 1992, and September 30, 1996, only 2.6 percent were found to have reasonable cause. This means the EEOC investigation determined that discrimination occurred based on evidence obtained in the investigation. Over 46 percent of the cases were found to have no reasonable cause; in those cases the EEOC determined that based on the evidence obtained, discrimination did not appear to have occurred. Merit resolution occurred in approximately 14 percent of the cases. This means the complaint was settled with a negotiated settlement, withdrawal with benefits, and/or successful or unsuccessful conciliation. During the period represented in Table 2.1, $116,983,166 was paid in benefits under Title I of the ADA to employees who had filed complaints based on discrimination because of disabilities. This figure suggests the stakes are high when employers violate Title I of the ADA.

CONCLUSIONS

In this chapter, the technical aspects of Title I are presented. Title I is critical to social work agencies because it deals with the employment provisions of the ADA. This chapter covers the basic components of Title

I; offers questions and answers related to the employment of people with disabilities; and suggests questions that should be used when interviewing persons with disabilities, as well as other critical information.

Title I is extremely complex because each disability case must be viewed as unique. Even though a number of clear answers can be given for certain questions related to Title I, many times they cannot. For example, a reasonable accommodation for a person with a disability in the workplace often calls for creativity and patience by the employer. No two reasonable-accommodation requests are alike because each worker with a disability is different; each workplace is different. Problems related to dealing with psychiatric disabilities are also extremely complex, as illustrated in this chapter. One must keep in mind, however, that dealing with other kinds of disabilities under the ADA is really no less complex than dealing with emotional impairments.

Title I is extremely important to professional social workers. It is critical that practitioners know this law; not knowing the provisions of this law can be very costly. Professional social workers also have an obligation to understand Title I because they often are involved in advocacy efforts for persons with disabilities. Advocacy and the ADA are the focus of Chapter 6.

REFERENCES

American Psychiatric Association. (1994). *Diagnostic and statistical manual of mental disorders: DSM IV (4th edn.)*. Washington, D.C.: American Psychiatric Association.

Bennett-Alexander, D. L., and Pincus, L. B. (1985). *Employment law for business*. Chicago: Irwin.

Equal Employment Opportunity Commission. (1997). *EEOC enforcement guidance: The American With Disabilities Act and psychiatric disabilities*. Washington, D.C.: Government Printing Office.

Equal Employment Opportunity Commission and U.S. Department of Justice. (1992). *The Americans With Disabilities Act: Questions and answers*. Washington, D.C.: National Institute on Disabilities and Rehabilitation Research.

Great Plains Disability and Business Technical Assistance Center. (1995). *Americans With Disabilities Act technical assistance manual Title II*. Columbia, MO: Great Plains Disability and Business Technical Assistance Center.

TADAR: The ADA Report (1997). Vol. 6, No. 1. Columbia: University of Missouri.

Chapter 3

Technical Aspects of Title II

Title II of the ADA prohibits discrimination against persons with disabilities in all services, programs, and activities provided or made available by state or local government. Public colleges and universities fall under the requirements of Title II. As pointed out in Chapter 1, Title II of the ADA extends the nondiscrimination requirements of Section 504 to the activities of all state and local governments, regardless of whether they receive any federal support (Veres and Sims, 1995). Title II has two subtitles, A and B. Subtitle A covers all activities of state and local governments other than public transit. Subtitle B deals with the provision of publicly funded transit. The focus of this chapter is on Subtitle A of Title II.

ACTIVITIES COVERED UNDER TITLE II

Title II covers every type of state or local government activity or program. In employment, state and local governments cannot discriminate against job applicants and employees with disabilities regardless of the number of people they employ (Veres and Sims, 1995).

Title II covers the following types of programs and activities: (1) Activities and programs involving general public contact, including communication with the public through telephone contact, office walk-ins, and interviews;

and (2) Activities and programs directly administered by state and local government for beneficiaries and participants including programs that provide state or local government services and benefits.

Under Title II, in order to be protected, a person must be a "qualified individual with a disability." A qualified individual with a disability is defined as a person who, with or without reasonable modifications to rules, policies, and practices, meets the essential eligibility requirements for the receipt of services or the participation in programs or activities provided by a state or local government (Adoptive Environments Centers, 1992).

Subtitle A of Title II has a number of basic requirements critical to public-supported social work agencies. These also apply to all activities and programs of state or local governments. Furthermore, if a state or local government enters into a contract with a private entity, it must ensure that the activity operated under contract is in compliance with Title II. As discussed in Chapter 1, the following are basic requirements under Title II. Illustrations are offered under each requirement (The Great Plains Disability and Business Technical Assistance Center, 1995).

1. Integrated Setting

Integration is the fundamental component of Title II. State or local governments that fail to fully integrate people with disabilities into programs and services violate Title II.

Illustration: A public school of social work cannot refuse to admit an individual to a forum that is open to the public merely because the individual is deaf. In fact, an interpreter would probably have to be provided by the school if the person who is deaf requests this accommodation.

Illustration: An individual who uses a wheelchair will not have equal opportunity to participate in a program if applications must be filed in a second-floor office of a building without an elevator, because he or she would not be able to reach the office.

2. Participation in Separate Programs

Under Title II, state and local governments can offer programs that are specifically designed for people with disabilities; however, they cannot be forced to participate in such programs.

Illustration: Museums generally do not allow visitors to touch exhibits because handling can damage objects. A municipal museum may offer a special tour for individuals with vision impairments during which they are permitted to touch and handle specific objects on a limited basis.

Illustration: A city recreational department may sponsor a separate basketball league for individuals who use wheelchairs.

Illustration: A school system should provide wheelchair access at its schools so that children who use wheelchairs can attend school at locations comparable in convenience to those available to other children. Also, where "magnet" schools, or schools offering different curricula or instruction techniques, are available, the range of choice provided to students with disabilities must be comparable to that offered to other students.

3. Right to Refuse an Accommodation

A person with a disability does not have to accept an accommodation if he or she so chooses.

Illustration: A museum's special program for those with vision impairments can be refused by individuals with this impairment. If they so choose, they can take the standard museum tour.

4. Accommodation to the Regular Program

If a person with a disability decides not to participate in a special program, the state or local government is obligated to provide accommodations for that individual to benefit from the regular program.

Illustration: If a museum provides a sign-language interpreter for one of its regularly scheduled tours, the availability of the signed tour may be a factor in determining whether it would be an undue burden to provide an interpreter for a deaf person who wants to take the tour at a different time. However, the availability of the signed tour would not affect the museum's obligation to provide an interpreter for a different tour, or the museum's obligation to provide a different auxiliary aid, such as an assistive listening device, for an individual with impaired hearing who does not use sign language.

5. Eligibility Criteria That Screen Out People With Disabilities

It is discrimination for a state or local government to apply eligibility criteria or standards that screen out or tend to screen out individuals with disabilities.

Illustration: The director of a county recreation program prohibits people who use wheelchairs from participating in county-sponsored scuba diving classes because he believes that people who use wheelchairs probably cannot swim well enough to participate. An unnecessary blanket exclusion of this nature would violate Title II.

Illustration: A community college requires students with certain disabilities to be accompanied to class by attendants, even when such individuals prefer to attend classes unaccompanied. The college also requires individuals with disabilities to provide extensive medical histories, although such histories are not required from other students. Unless the college can demonstrate that it is necessary for some compelling reason to adopt these policies, the policies would not be permitted by Title II.

6. Modifications in Policies

Reasonable modifications in policies and practices, and procedures when such modifications are necessary to avoid discrimination on the basis of disability, are required under Title II.

Illustration: A municipal zoning ordinance requires a setback of twelve feet from the curb in the central business district. In order to install a ramp to the front entrance of a pharmacy, the owner must encroach on the setback by three feet. Granting a variance in the zoning may be a reasonable modification of town policy.

Illustration: A county general relief program provides emergency food, shelter, and cash grants to individuals who can demonstrate their eligibility. The application process, however, is extremely lengthy and complex. When many individuals with mental disabilities apply for benefits, they are unable to complete the application successfully. As a result, they are effectively denied benefits to which they are entitled. In this case, the county has an obligation to make reasonable modifications to its application process to ensure that otherwise eligible individuals are not denied needed benefits. Modifications to the relief program might include simplifying the application process or providing applicants who have mental disabilities with individualized assistance to complete the process.

Illustration: A social work student in a state-supported school has an environmental illness. She requests that the School adopt a policy prohibiting the use of perfume or other scented products by other students who come into contact with her. Such a requirement is probably not a reasonable modification of school policy.

7. Association

It is discrimination under Title II for a state or local government to exclude or deny equal services, programs, or activities to an individual or entity because of the known disability of another individual with whom the individual or entity has a relationship or association.

Illustration: A county recreation center may not refuse admission to a summer camp program to a child whose brother has AIDS.

Illustration: A local government could not refuse to allow a theater company to use a school auditorium on the grounds that the company recently performed at an AIDS hospice.

Illustration: A state-supported school of social work refuses to admit Ed to its MSW program because he has AIDS. The school also refuses to admit his friend, Dan, who does not have AIDS. The school would be discriminating against Dan because of his association with Ed. The school is also discriminating against Ed because he was refused admission because of his disability, AIDS.

8. Surcharges

A state or local government cannot impose a surcharge on an individual with a disability or on a group of individuals with disabilities to cover the cost of measures taken to comply with the ADA.

Illustration: A public-supported school of social work provides interpreter services to a deaf student, removes a limited number of architectural barriers, and relocates inaccessible courses and activities to more accessible locations. The school cannot place a surcharge on either an individual student with a disability (such as a deaf student who benefited from interpreter services) or on groups of students with disabilities (such as students with mobility impairments who benefited form barrier removal). It may, however, adjust its tuition or fees for all students.

9. Granting Licenses and Certifications

Under Title II, a state or local government cannot discriminate against a qualified individual with a disability, on the basis of the disability, in granting licenses and certifications.

Illustration: The state oversees a day care facility-licensing law. State policy requires day care center staff to be physically mobile. This policy discriminates against teachers with mobility-related disabilities and thus violates Title II.

10. Protection Against Retaliation

Under Title II, persons who file complaints are protected from retaliation and harassment.

Illustration: A master of social work student files a charge of discrimination against the dean of a state school of social work. If the dean has the student removed from the program because of the complaint, the dean has illegally retaliated against the student and has violated Title II.

Illustration: A professor of social work in a state-supported social work program reduces a student's grade because she testified in a Title II grievance proceeding against the school of social work. The professor has illegally retaliated against the student.

QUESTIONS AND ANSWERS ON TITLE II

The following questions and answers will help professional social workers better understand the technical aspects of Title II. The information is based on materials published by the EEOC and the U.S. Department of Justice (Equal Employment Opportunity Commission and U.S. Department of Justice, 1992).

Question: What is a self-evaluation?

Answer: A self-evaluation is a public entity's assessment of its policies and practices. The self-evaluation identifies and corrects those policies and practices that are inconsistent with Title II's requirements. A public entity that employs fifty or more employees must retain its self-evaluation for three years. Other public entities are not required to retain their self-evaluations, but are encouraged to do so because these documents evidence a public entity's good-faith efforts to comply with Title II requirements.

Question: What does Title II require for new construction and alterations?

Answer: Title II requires that all new buildings constructed by a state or local government be accessible. In addition, when a state or local government undertakes alterations to a building, it must make the altered portions accessible.

Question: How will a state or local government know that a new building is accessible?

Answer: A state or local government will be in compliance with the ADA for new construction and alterations if it follows one of two accessibility standards. It can choose the *Uniform Federal Accessibility Guidelines for Buildings and Facilities*, which is the standard that must be used for public accommodations and commercial facilities under Title III of the ADA. If the state or local government chooses the *ADA Accessibility Guidelines*, it is not entitled to the elevator exemption (which permits certain private buildings under three stories or under 3,000 square feet per floor to be constructed without an elevator).

Question: What requirements apply to a public entity's emergency telephone services, such as 911?

Answer: State and local agencies that provide emergency telephone services must provide "direct access" to individuals who rely on a TDD or a computer modem for telephone communication. Telephone access through a third party or through a relay service does not satisfy the requirement for direct access. Where a public entity provides 911 telephone service, it may not substitute a separate seven-digit telephone line as the sole means for access to 911 services by non-voice users. A public entity may, however, provide a separate seven-digit line for the exclusive use of non-voice callers in addition to providing direct access for such calls to its 911 line.

Question: Does Title II require that telephone emergency service systems be compatible with all formats used for non-voice communications?

Answer: No, telephone emergency services must only be compatible with the Baudot format. The Baudot format converts letters to acoustic signals and sends them over a conventional telephone line which then converts it back to text to be read on a display monitor. Until it can be proved that communications in another format can operate in a reliable and compatible manner in a given telephone emergency environment, a public entity is not required to provide direct access to computer modems using formats other than Baudot.

Question: How are Title II requirements for state and local governments enforced?

Answer: Private individuals may sue to enforce their rights under Title II and may receive the same remedies as those provided under Section 504 of the Rehabilitation Act of 1973, including reasonable attorney's fees. Individuals may also file complaints with eight designated federal agencies, including the U.S. Department of Justice and the Department of Education.

ADA CHECKLIST

The following checklist provides the professional social worker with information on the kinds of activities that are allowed under Title II. Statements that are answered with a no should alert the agency to modify its practice.

1. No standards, methods of administration, or criteria are used that discriminate on the basis of disability by the facility or its contractors.
   Yes ———   No ———

2. Association or relationship with a person with a disability is not the basis for denial of goods, services, privileges, advantages, accommodations, or opportunities.
   Yes ———   No ———

3. Eligibility criteria that are not necessary for the provision of a service, privilege, advantage, or accommodation are not used.
   Yes ———   No ———

4. No criteria, not applied to others, will serve to limit the participation of an individual with a disability.
   Yes ———   No ———

5. Readily achievable methods are used to remove architectural barriers.
   Yes ———   No ———

6. Readily achievable methods are used to remove communication barriers.
   Yes ———   No ———

7. When barriers cannot readily be removed from facilities, alternative means are employed.
   Yes ———   No ———

8. When major structural renovations are made, the altered path of travel, rest rooms, telephones, and drinking fountains are accessible to and usable by individuals with disabilities.
   Yes ———   No ———

9. Buildings constructed after January 26, 1993, are readily accessible to and usable by individuals with disabilities.
   Yes ———   No ———

10. Vehicles purchased by the facility after August 26, 1990, that carry more than seven passengers (including the driver) provide level entry or a wheelchair lift with securement devices.

Yes ———   No ———

PUBLIC ACCOMMODATIONS

Public accommodations are covered under Title III. Many of the provisions of Title III are similar to those of Title II; however, they apply to private entities. Privately operated entities offering certain types of courses and examinations, privately operated transportation, and commercial facilities are covered by Title III. Private universities offering social work programs also fall under Title III. It should be noted that private universities receiving federal funding also must comply with Section 504 of the 1973 Rehabilitation Act. As covered in Chapter 1, Section 504 requirements are almost identical to those of Title II of the ADA. In other words, private universities offering social work programs have nearly identical requirements concerning the treatment of students with disabilities as public universities do because of Section 504.

The requirements under Title III mean private entities must comply with basic nondiscrimination requirements that prohibit exclusion, segregation, and unequal treatment of people with disabilities. Under Title III, private entities must comply with architectural standards for new and altered buildings; they must make reasonable modifications to policies, practices, and procedures to help ensure that people with disabilities have access to programs and services they offer (Equal Employment Opportunity Commission and U.S. Department of Justice, 1992).

Under Title III, courses and examinations related to professional or trade-related applications, licensing, certifications, or credentialing must be provided in a place and manner accessible to people with disabilities, or alternative accessible arrangements must be offered. In education, this means that testing by private agencies of students must make appropriate accommodations for test takers who have disabilities (Equal Employment Opportunity Commission and U.S. Department of Justice, 1992).

Complaints of Title III violations may be filed with the Department of Justice. In certain situations, cases may be referred to a mediation program sponsored by this department. The Department of Justice is authorized to sue where there is a pattern or practice of discrimination in violation of Title III, or where an act of discrimination raises an issue of general public importance. Title III may also be enforced through private lawsuits. It is not necessary to file a complaint with the Department of Justice in order to receive a "right-to-sue" letter. A "right-to-sue" letter allows a complainant to sue in federal court (Equal Employment Opportunity Commission and U.S. Department of Justice, 1992).

While this chapter focuses on Title II, it is important to note that Titles II and III have similar requirements. Title II, however, covers public entities, while Title III covers private entities. Professional social workers should be familiar with the provisions of both Titles II and III because they mandate requirements concerning the treatment of people with disabilities in the public and private sectors. Social workers work and deliver services in both of these sectors. Furthermore, knowledge of the provisions under both titles will help social workers to become more effective advocates for people with disabilities.

CONCLUSIONS

This chapter covers the technical requirements of Title II. Like other titles under the ADA, it is difficult to establish rules and procedures that will neatly cover all ADA-related problems and issues. At best, this chapter provides a general technical guide to Title II. The relationship of Title II and Title III is also covered.

As noted in this chapter, Title II prohibits discrimination against persons with disabilities in all services, programs, and activities provided or made available by state or local government. State and local governments were prohibited from discriminating against persons with disabilities prior to the ADA under Section 504 of the Rehabilitation Act of 1973. Section 504 prohibits discrimination on the basis of disability in any programs and activities that receive a set amount of federal funding. Section 504 applies to social work programs that are part of private universities receiving federal funds. The requirements of Title II and Section 504 are similar; therefore, social work programs in public and private universities have requirements that are almost identical for the treatment of students with disabilities.

REFERENCES

Adaptive Environments Center Inc. (1992). *ADA Title II action guide*. Horsham, PA: Axon Group.

Equal Employment Opportunity Commission and U.S. Department of Justice. (1992). *The Americans With Disabilities Act: Questions and answers*. Washington, DC: National Institute on Disabilities and Rehabilitation Research.

Great Plains Disability and Business Technical Assistance Center. (1995). *Americans With Disabilities Act technical assistance manual Title II*. Columbia, MO: Great Plains Disability and Business Technical Assistance Center.

Veres, J. G., and Sims, R. R. (eds.) (1995). *Human resources management and the Americans With Disabilities Act*. Westport, CT: Quorum Books.

Chapter 4

Social Work Agencies and the Americans With Disabilities Act

Social work agencies, public and private, are bound by the regulations of Title I (Employment Provisions) of the ADA. The only agencies that do not have to follow Title I procedures in employment are those that employ fewer than fifteen people. All public social work agencies must be in compliance with Title II (Nondiscrimination by State and Local Governments); private agencies are governed by Title III (Public Accommodations). This chapter presents the impact that the ADA has had on social work agencies. Areas covered include employment rights of people with disabilities in social work settings and the rights of clients with disabilities. As in other parts of this book, examples are provided to help the reader better understand the legal requirements of the ADA.

DISABILITY RIGHTS

Federal equal employment opportunity (EEO) laws prohibit employment discrimination on the basis of race, color, religion, sex, and age. With the passage of the Rehabilitation Act of 1973 and the Americans With Disabilities Act in 1990, people with disabilities were extended protection from employment discrimination; they are the most recent disadvantaged group to receive this protection.

The Rehabilitation Act of 1973 was the first major federal law protecting people with disabilities from discrimination. People with disabilities were provided with EEO rights specifically in the federal government and in public and private programs funded and contracted by or with the federal government. Sections 503 and 504 for the first time created EEO rights for people with disabilities in the private sector, but only if a private organization received federal support. The Small Business Administration estimated that over five million businesses in 1991 were bound by the mandates of the Rehabilitation Act because they received federal support (Fersh and Thomas, 1993). The passage of the Americans With Disabilities Act extended coverage to more people with disabilities, because many private and public organizations must follow the mandates of this new law even though they do not receive federal support. The protection for people with disabilities under the ADA is similar to that extended to other protected groups.

Eighty-seven percent of America's private-sector jobs are covered under Title I of the ADA. All businesses and nonprofit associations, with some exceptions, that employ fifteen or more people cannot discriminate on the basis of disability in any phase of employment (Fersh and Thomas, 1993). The Equal Employment Opportunity Commission enforces the employment provisions under the ADA. Other aspects of the ADA also protect people with disabilities from other kinds of discrimination.

DEFINITION OF A DISABILITY

As covered in Chapter 1, the term "disability" as defined by the ADA is "a physical or mental impairment that substantially limits one or more major life activities." This definition is based on the one used in the Rehabilitation Act of 1973; however, the ADA uses the more widely accepted term "disability" rather than "handicap." For an individual to be defined as disabled under the ADA, he or she must meet one or more of the following criteria (Americans With Disabilities Act P.L. 101–336, 1990: 6):

1. Has a physical or mental impairment that substantially limits one or more major life activities.

2. Has a record of such an impairment.

3. Is regarded as having such an impairment.

Major life activities include but are not limited to walking, speaking, seeing, hearing, breathing, learning, working, and caring for oneself.

The ADA does not offer a list of specific disabilities covered by this new law. The reason for not developing a list is provided in a 1989 report (*The Americans With Disabilities Act of 1989: 22*) from the U.S. Senate:

> It is not possible to include in the [ADA] legislation a list of all the specific conditions, diseases, or infections that would constitute physical or mental impairments because of the difficulty of ensuring the comprehensiveness of such a list, particularly in light of the fact that new disorders may develop in the future. The term includes, however, such conditions, diseases, and infections as orthopedic, visual, speech, and hearing impairment, cerebral palsy, epilepsy, muscular dystrophy, multiple sclerosis, infections with the human immunodeficiency virus (HIV), cancer, heart disease, diabetes, mental retardation, emotional illness, and specific learning disabilities.

The definition of a disability under the ADA includes individuals who have recovered from a physical or mental impairment that previously substantially limited a major life activity. Individuals regarded by others as being disabled and those who associate with people with disabilities are covered by the ADA.

Conditions that are not defined as disabilities include homosexuality, illegal drug use, and economic or cultural disadvantage. However, if a person is currently dependent on alcohol or has a history of alcohol dependency, he or she is covered by the ADA. An individual who has a history of illegal drug use and is no longer using drugs is protected by the ADA.

EMPLOYMENT RIGHTS

Social workers must be particularly knowledgeable of the employment rights of people with disabilities. These rights are designed to help people with disabilities to become equal partners and equal members in the work force. With this new equality, people with disabilities can strive, like other Americans, to obtain jobs that meet their needs and talents.

The ADA has an umbrella effect on almost every employment decision made in a social work agency covered by its provisions. These include hiring, promotions, firings, and fringe benefits. The rights of people with disabilities are grounded in the Human Rights philosophy discussed earlier in this book. This means people with disabilities have a right to dignity and respect, and to be treated on the basis of merit regardless of their disabilities.

The following are the basic employment rights of people with disabilities (Fersh and Thomas, 1993).

1. The right not to be discriminated against on the basis of a disability in employment decisions.

   The ADA is very clear on employment discrimination. Simply put, an employer cannot discriminate against a qualified applicant or an employee on the basis of a disability. The ADA prohibits discrimination in all aspects of the employment process. Prior to the ADA's enactment, many people with disabilities were denied even job interviews because they had disabilities.

2. The right not to be discriminated against on the basis of being regarded as having a disability.

   The ADA prohibits discrimination on the basis of being regarded as having a disability. Prior to passage of the ADA, an employer could fire an employee simply if the employee was regarded as having a disability. For example, even after passage of the ADA, employees have been fired because co-workers felt they had AIDS. This behavior by an employer is a violation of the ADA.

3. Employees with disabilities have a right to be judged on their own merits.

   The ADA requires that job applicants or employees with disabilities be judged on their abilities and not on their physical or mental impairments. For example, cancer survivors are protected by the ADA even after they have been cured of the disease. It is not unusual for employers to discriminate against a productive cancer survivor on the basis that the cancer will return (Pardeck, 1996). This means the cancer survivor is being judged on his or her history of a disability and not on merit.

4. The right not to be screened out of employment opportunities because of a disability.

   This right means that the person with a disability cannot be excluded from a job unless the person cannot do the essential job requirements. If a test or standard is used to exclude a person with a disability, it must be shown that the standard is job-related. For example, if a social work agency has a rule that all employees must have a valid driver's license, this rule would screen out blind applicants for positions in the agency. The agency must clearly be able to show, if challenged by a complainant, that the driver's license requirement is an essential function of all positions in the organization.

5. The right to reveal to an employer an emotional or physical impairment without being discriminated against.

   Some disabilities are hidden; these include learning disabilities and epilepsy. Job applicants often do not feel comfortable revealing these kinds of disabilities because of discrimination. People with a learning disability may have to tell a potential employer that they have such an impairment and that they can do all of the essential functions of a position with a reasonable accommodation. When an applicant or an employee reveals that he or she has a disability, this person is protected from job discrimination based on the disability.

6. The right to be tested and evaluated fairly.

   An individual with a disability that impairs sensory, manual, or speaking skills has the right to take an appropriate test that measures his or her true abilities. This means it is unlawful to administer a test to a job applicant who is not capable of taking the test because of an impairment. For example, if a clinical social worker with dyslexia applies for a position in an agency, the agency will probably have to provide the applicant with a reader for a test that all applicants have to complete. If the person is hired, he or she may have to be provided with a reader or some other reasonable accommodation that allows this person to understand instructions through a medium other than writing. People with certain kinds of disabilities may be able to have a fair evaluation of job skill potential only if they receive a reasonable accommodation such as a reader. If an employer does not provide the accommodation, and it is not deemed to be an undue hardship, the ADA has probably been violated.

7. The right to request and to be provided with reasonable accommodation.

   At times an employer may have to provide a job applicant or employee with a reasonable accommodation. This accommodation helps to level the playing field in employment for the person with a disability. Most accommodations requested by people with disabilities are inexpensive; some are not (Great Plains Disability and Business Technical Assistance Center, 1995). If the employer feels the accommodation creates an undue hardship, the accommodation can be refused; however, this action may then be challenged by a job applicant or employee. Reasonable accommodations include: part-time or modified work schedules, job restructuring, job reassignment, provision of auxiliary aids and services, and modifications to a job site or work site.

8. The right not to be disqualified for a job based on the inability to perform a nonessential job function.

All jobs have essential functions that an applicant or employee must be able to do. An employer is not required to hire or retain an employee who cannot do these essential functions successfully. However, if the person has a disability, and that disability prevents him or her from doing an essential job function, the employer must provide a reasonable accommodation that allows the person to perform an essential function. If this cannot be accomplished successfully, an employee may be terminated.

Many jobs, however, have nonessential functions, such as answering a phone. For example, a clinical social worker may have some form of physical impairment that prevents him from answering the phone; this job function may well be assigned to another person. The ADA requires that an employee cannot be terminated because he is unable to perform a nonessential job function.

9. The right not to be limited, segregated, or classified as an individual with a disability.

People with disabilities have a right to equal job opportunity; this means an employer cannot limit, segregate, or classify a job applicant or an employee in such a way that prevents equal job opportunity. For example, a rule that no one with a history of emotional disability can apply for clinical social work positions in an agency is a violation of the ADA. Such behavior by an employer would be similar to having a standard for employment that no people of color are eligible for clinical social work positions. In fact, when social work agencies have sensitivity training that focuses on issues related to cultural diversity, it is recommended that the topic of disabilities be a part of the training.

10. The right not to be asked about a disability in a job interview or on a job application.

   The ADA is clear on this right. An employer cannot ask a job applicant in any form about a disabling condition he or she may have. Prior to the passage of the ADA, employers often used the information about an applicant's disabilities as reason for not hiring her. This was particularly true for people with hidden disabilities such as epilepsy, diabetes, emotional illness, and cancer. A social work agency should note that it has no right to inquire about a job applicant's disability or history of a disability for any position within an agency. For example, a clinical social worker who applies for a therapist's position in a social work agency cannot be denied the position on the basis that she has gone through treatment for chemical dependency. As long as the applicant is not using illegal drugs and has successfully completed a treatment program, she is protected by the ADA.

11. The right not to be required to undergo a medical examination before being offered a job.

   Under the ADA, in most circumstances, a job applicant cannot be required to take a medical exam prior to being offered a job. After a job is offered, the employer can require a medical examination. The only limited circumstance in which an employer may conduct a medical examination during the application process is if the employer can clearly demonstrate that such pre-employment inquiries are related to performing an essential job function. Such pre-employment inquiries would be very difficult to justify within the field of social work.

12. The right for employees with disabilities to receive equal access to health and life insurance and other job benefits.

   Employees with disabilities have the right to receive the same benefits as other employees. A person with a disability cannot be required to pay higher insurance premiums for group health insurance because of a disability. One of the core reasons for job discrimination against survivors of serious illnesses such as cancer is that employers feel such illnesses will drive up insurance costs. A new federal law that complements the ADA is the Health Insurance Portability and Accountability Act (HIPAA) (1996).

HIPAA also mandates that employers cannot deny health insurance to employees because they have medical conditions.

13. The right not to be discriminated against as a threat to safety or health, unless the employer meets certain standards required by law.

    A person who is HIV positive or has AIDS and is a qualified employee or job applicant cannot be discriminated against because of these conditions. Another excellent example for social work agencies would be the person who is able to control a psychiatric condition through medication and is able to do his or her job. This person cannot be discriminated against because of the psychiatric impairment. A clinical social worker who controls a psychiatric condition through medication and is qualified for an agency position cannot be discriminated against on the basis of the emotional impairment.

14. The right not to be retaliated against.

    Under the ADA, a person who invokes his or her rights under the act is protected from retaliation. This includes persons who may not be disabled, but file complaints on behalf of people with disabilities. An example of this kind of action is included under the situational analysis offered in this chapter.

15. The right not to be discriminated against because one is associated with a person with a disability.

    Employers have discriminated against qualified applicants or employees because they have an association with a person with a disability. An example of this would be a social work agency that refuses to hire a qualified clinical social worker because he or she is married to a person who is in treatment for cancer. The agency may refuse to hire the applicant based on the belief that the person will have to take off days to care for the spouse in treatment or the applicant's spouse will drive up health insurance costs under the agency's family group plan. This kind of behavior by an employer is discrimination under the ADA.

EXAMPLES OF WHAT EMPLOYERS CANNOT DO

Supervisors and employees in social work agencies must realize that a number of practices often used during the hiring process is no longer legal under the ADA. For example, it was a common practice to ask job applicants about their medical histories; this is no longer legal. The following list from the *Americans With Disabilities Act Handbook* (Equal Employment Opportunity Commission and U.S. Department of Justice, 1991: Section vii, pp. 2–3) covers activities employers cannot do.

1. An employer cannot use an application form that lists a number of disabilities, asks how an individual became disabled or the prognosis of the disability, or how often the individual will need treatment or leave as a result of the disability. However, the employer may state the attendance requirements of the job and ask the applicant if this requirement can be met.

2. An otherwise qualified person with a disability cannot be disqualified for a position because of the individual's inability to perform nonessential or marginal functions of the job.

3. Employers are required to make employment decisions based on facts applicable to individual applicants or employees and not on the basis of presumptions as to what a class of individuals with disabilities can or cannot do.

4. An employer cannot limit the duties of an individual with a disability based on a presumption of what is best for the individual or about the ability of the individual to perform certain tasks.

5. Employers cannot deny an applicant employment based on generalized fears about the safety of the applicant or higher rates of absenteeism.

6. An employer cannot deny a qualified individual with a disability equal access to health and life insurance, or subject the person to different terms of insurance based on the disability alone, if the disability does not impose increased risks.

7. Employers cannot administer employment tests to applicants or employees who have sensory, manual, or speaking impairments in formats that require the use of the impaired skill.

8. It is unlawful for an employer to use standards, criteria, or methods of administration that are not job-related and consistent with business necessity and that have the effect of discriminating or perpetuating discrimination.

9. Employers cannot restrict the employment opportunities, or segregate into separate work areas or into separate lines of advancement, qualified individuals with disabilities based on stereotypes and myths about an individual's disability.

10. An employer cannot deny employment to an individual with a disability because of a slightly increased risk to the health or safety of the individual or others. The risk can only be considered when it poses a significant risk or high probability of substantial harm. A speculative or remote risk is insufficient.

SITUATIONAL ANALYSES

The situational analyses below will help supervisors and other agency personnel increase their understanding of the requirements of the ADA in the workplace. The following examples (except situations 4 and 5) are based on cases offered by J. G. Allen (1994) and have been substantially revised to fit potential issues related to the ADA in social work agencies.

Situation 1

A religious-based social work agency wants to hire only social workers of its faith. Edward L. uses a wheelchair and does not practice the same religion as the one on which the agency is based. He's a highly qualified social worker, and no other qualified social workers have applied for the position. Can Edward L. use the ADA to compel the agency to hire him?

Analysis: No, Edward L. can't use the ADA to get the position. The ADA upholds religious autonomy, and Edward can be denied employment because his beliefs are inconsistent with the agency's. However, if Edward can prove he was rejected because of his disability (as by the hiring of someone without a disability who has religious beliefs other than the agency's), the agency would probably lose this defense. This exception to the ADA pertains only to religious organizations and only to employment.

Situation 2

Connie P. is a medical social worker in a hospital setting. She had a laryngectomy and uses a hand-held electronic voice box. She has applied for a promotion to a supervisory position. The hospital refuses to promote Connie because the union contract states that promotions may be given only to employees who are "able to fully perform all functions of the job." A supervisor must be able to use the hospital paging system for emergencies.

One of Connie's nondisabled co-workers with less experience wants the job. Can Connie use the ADA as a basis for persuading her employer to ignore the contract? Can she enforce her right to a promotion if the employer refuses to promote her? Must she research workplace alternatives herself?

Analysis: Connie can credibly argue that the ADA pre-empts the collective bargaining agreement. Even specific duties written into the contract will be construed liberally in her favor. Only essential duties are likely to survive government or court scrutiny. That means Connie can enforce her right to the promotion if some practical solution ("reasonable accommodation") to the paging problem can be found.

Connie has no legal duty to research the matter, but doing so would increase her chances of successfully confronting the employer. She should consult her union official and follow the contract grievance procedure. The various paging technologies available, such as whistles, bells, and lights, should persuade the hospital to promote Connie forthwith.

Situation 3

Sharon H. is a nondisabled supervisor in a social work agency who witnessed discrimination against another supervisor with a disability. When a charge of discrimination was filed, the Equal Employment Opportunity Commission contacted Sharon to assist its investigation. The agency policy manual states that supervisors are expected to protect agency interest at all times. Sharon wants to cooperate with the EEOC but fears retaliation by her employer. Is there any protection for her? Does the ADA prevent mistreatment on the job as well as termination?

Analysis: Yes, Sharon is fully protected against any retaliation on the job. It is unlawful for an employer to take negative action against someone who participates in an investigation of discriminatory practices. It makes no difference whether such practices actually occurred. Sharon is protected even if she just states her opposition to such practices. But, as a supervisor, she is in an excellent position to do something positive about the discrimination.

Discrimination is often the result of insensitivity or ignorance. At a management meeting, Sharon might suggest discussing the issue. The local EEOC or state rehabilitation agency might be able to provide a guest speaker at no charge. She could circulate copies of materials from the U.S. Justice Department or the EEOC concerning the ADA. An excellent example of this kind of material is *The Americans With Disabilities Act: Questions and Answers* (Equal Employment Opportunity Commission and the U.S. Department of Justice, 1992).

Situation 4

Michael J., a social worker in a large state agency, files a discrimination complaint with the EEOC claiming he was denied a promotion because he has a history of cancer. His supervisor calls Michael into his office and states that the complaint will affect the organization's morale and that he cannot understand why Michael wants to sue the agency. The supervisor tells Michael he will announce at the next staff meeting that Michael has filed a complaint so co-workers can talk to Michael about it. The supervisor announces that Michael filed a complaint the following week at a staff meeting.

Analysis: The fact that the supervisor talked to Michael about the complaint can be seen as retaliation. The announcement of the complaint in a group setting (staff meeting) provides further documentation of retaliation. The announcement of the complaint also violates the ADA because confidential medical information was released; the staff members now know Michael has a history of cancer. A history of cancer is covered under the ADA, and someone with a history of cancer is protected from discrimination throughout his or her working career.

Situation 5

During the search for a new social worker to fill an agency position, an employee of the agency informs the search committee that two of the applicants have a history of medical problems. Specifically, the employee states that one applicant had a heart attack and the other applicant is in remission, implying that this applicant's disability is alcoholism.

Analysis: The rights of both applicants have been violated under the ADA. The employee who offered this information concerning the two applicants should be reported to the agency's affirmative action officer.

Situation 6

A social worker's supervisor notices the worker is losing hair and looks tired; the supervisor asks the employee to undergo a medical exam for cancer within the next month.

Analysis: The supervisor has violated the ADA.

Situation 7

Mary D., a social worker with a disability requiring a wheelchair, has been asked to attend a convention sponsored by the agency. She has learned that the hotel holding the convention doesn't have wheelchair access. The only way she can attend is to be carried around by two people. Does the ADA cover Mary in this situation? How should she approach the agency about the access issue?

Analysis: Mary is definitely covered in this situation. Even if a meeting planner or other outside contractor is arranging the convention for the employer, ADA regulations fully apply. The agency has a duty to require compliance by the hotel and by all transportation, meeting, lodging, and eating facilities connected with the event.

Because the hotel (and other entities used during the trip) must comply with the ADA, Mary might suggest that her agency use this as a reason to change locations. The agency will then be on notice that it is participating in violation of a potent federal law.

Situation 8

James L. has one arm. He wants to apply for a position in a large social work agency. The position involves working with computer technology. His resume says "Health: Excellent." When the agency calls him for an interview, he becomes concerned that the health statement on his resume will cause him to lose his protection under the ADA.

When the agency calls him for an interview, James observes that the computer equipment he must work with can be easily adapted to someone with one arm. Has James misrepresented his health? Can he be denied employment for not disclosing his disability? Must the agency allow him to show that he can use the equipment successfully?

Analysis: James has nothing to worry about; his health *is* excellent for a position involving work with computer technology. Even if he had several disabilities, the only issue is whether they are "job-related functional limitations."

Because using the equipment is an essential function of the position, it would appear reasonable under the circumstance for the employer to ask James how he would use the computer technology. His willingness to demonstrate would work in his favor.

Situation 9

Donna H. is a former drug addict with highly specialized experience in the treatment of alcoholics. She has said nothing about her drug history to the agency that offered her the best job of her life.

Donna later receives a confirming letter along with an eight-page document titled "Habitual Drug User Questionnaire." The questionnaire is to be completed and returned immediately. She had no idea it existed, and it was never mentioned during the interview. Colleagues have warned her the job offer will be revoked if she admits to a history of drug abuse.

Must Donna answer the questionnaire? Does she have to confess to her prior drug abuse? Should she contact the EEOC and file a charge of discrimination? Will that protect her job?

Analysis: Donna is protected against discrimination in employment based on her former drug addiction. Even someone enrolled in a drug rehabilitation program is protected.

She should not falsify the answers to the questionnaire. This employer's perceived "business necessity" can't justify discriminating against someone with a history of drug addiction. Donna (or her lawyer) should call the person who sent the questionnaire and tell him or her that it will be answered. Then the start date should be confirmed because Donna will definitely be reporting for work.

CLIENT RIGHTS

The ADA creates rights for clients with disabilities. These rights include access to and utilization of services and programs offered by social work agencies, as well as services offered by other entities. The rights of clients to services and programs offered by social work agencies fall under Titles II and III of the ADA (Fersh and Thomas, 1993). Chapter 5 will illustrate how these rights are also extended to social work students under these titles:

1. The right to access to and full utilization of programs and services offered by a social work agency.

   Clients have a right to access to the services of agencies if they are qualified individuals with disabilities. For example, if a client uses a wheelchair and is qualified for a particular service, the agency cannot deny the service because the person is unable to get into the building where the agency is housed. The agency must be accessible to people with disabilities who are qualified for a service or a program.

   Another example of this right would be the social work agency that offers field trips to low-income children as an enrichment program. The agency cannot deny children with an emotional or physical impairment access to the field trip because of their disability. Children with disabilities who qualify for services and programs offered have a right to participate in all of the agency's programs, including field trips.

2. Agencies cannot create policy that screens out or tends to screen out clients with disabilities.

This right applies not only to social work agencies, but also to services offered by other entities that the client with a disability may wish to use. For example, it can empower a client with a physical impairment to know that the ADA requires accessibility of programs and services offered by public and private entities. Professional social workers must teach their clients about these rights.

3. The right to access and utilize telecommunications.

Clients who are deaf or have hearing impairments have a right to fully utilize an agency's telephone system. Most of the responsibility for this right is met by the telecommunications systems that the agency uses. However, the social work agency does have some obligations related to clients who are deaf or who have hearing impairments that help ensure effective communication between the client and the agency.

4. The right to access and utilize public transportation.

This right is one in which the agency should provide educational programs to clients with disabilities that have traditionally prevented them from using public transportation. This strategy will empower clients because they will know the ADA requires their access to public transportation. Also, this is an excellent area in which professional social workers can serve as advocates for clients with emotional or physical impairments. The ADA requires that people with these kinds of disabilities have a right to public transportation unless it can be shown that they create a safety hazard to themselves or others.

PROVING DISCRIMINATION UNDER THE ADA

The following will focus on how employment discrimination is investigated under the ADA. A case will be offered to illustrate how the investigation process takes place by the EEOC (Adaptive Environments Center, 1992).

Defenses

The ADA identifies five basic defenses to a charge of employment discrimination on the basis of disability. The following list is not intended to be exhaustive.

1. *Disparate Treatment.* Disparate treatment means treating an individual differently on the basis of a disability. A defense to such a charge is that the alleged actions were based on legitimate, nondiscriminatory reasons that are not pretextual, such as an unsatisfactory job performance.

2. *Disparate Impact: Selection.* In this context, disparate impact means that selection criteria, although uniformly applied, have an adverse impact on people with disabilities. Such criteria are permissible only when job-related and consistent with business necessity and where no reasonable accommodation is available. Where selection criteria include a safety requirement that an individual not pose a direct threat, an employer must demonstrate that this requirement is job-related and consistent with business necessity.

3. *Disparate Impact: Nonselection.* Here, disparate impact means that nonselection criteria such as employer policies, although uniformly applied, have an adverse impact on persons with disabilities. As above, such criteria are permissible only when job-related and consistent with business necessity.

4. *Undue Hardship.* Undue hardship may be raised, for example, as a defense to a charge that an employer failed to provide a reasonable accommodation.

5. *Conflict With Other Federal Laws.* Where other federal laws may require or prohibit an action in conflict with the ADA requirements, the employer's obligation to comply with these conflicting standards may be raised as a defense.

The EEOC and the courts use the same legal proofs as those employed under Title VII for discrimination cases based on disability. The case law that has developed around legal rules related to the Rehabilitation Act of 1973 has also been the source for court decisions related to the ADA.

The well-known proof scheme resulting from *McDonnell Douglas v. Green* (1973) is often utilized for ADA employment-discrimination cases (Greenlaw and Kohl, 1996).

In this case, Green was laid off from his job when his employer, McDonnell Douglas, reduced its work force. Green was a longtime civil rights activist, and he subsequently charged that he was laid off because he was an African American.

In his protest against his former employer, Green attempted to block the plant's five main access roads during rush hour to prevent employees from entering. Green was arrested and fined for participating in the protest.

A few weeks after Green's protest and arrest, McDonnell Douglas advertised for "qualified mechanics"; Green applied. His application was rejected on the basis of his participation in the protest. Green filed a charge of discrimination with the EEOC, charging the company would not hire him because he was black.

Green's case eventually reached the U.S. Supreme Court. As a result of the appeal to the Supreme Court a schema of the proper order and nature of proofs in civil rights cases resulted. These are offered below.

Under *McDonnell Douglas*, a plaintiff must present a prima facie case. Establishing a prima facie case entails four steps. One, the plaintiff must show that he or she falls within a protected class. Green was black, and thus was protected by race. Second, the plaintiff must show he or she was qualified for a position. Third, the individual must be rejected for the position. Fourth, the plaintiff must show that he or she was rejected for the job and the employer continued to seek applicants with similar qualifications to the plaintiff's. If the prima facie case prevails, the employer must show a legitimate nondiscriminatory reason for rejecting the plaintiff. The plaintiff must then be given the opportunity to show the employer's nondiscriminatory reason was in fact a pretext for discrimination (Greenlaw and Kohl, 1996).

EXAMPLE OF AN ADA EMPLOYMENT DISCRIMINATION CASE

The following case focuses on a person with a hidden disability who alleged employment discrimination. Under the Americans With Disabilities Act, a disability is defined as a physical or mental impairment that substantially limits one or more of the major life activities of an individual, a record of such an impairment, or being regarded as having an impairment. Hidden disabilities often fall under the second prong of the ADA disability definition, a history of an impairment. The focus of this example is a person who had a history of cancer and was denied a promotion to an administrative position. A person who has a history of cancer is fully protected under the Americans With Disabilities Act. After reviewing the case, the *McDonnell Douglas v. Green* proof scheme will be applied to it.

Cancer and Employment Discrimination

Most people do not realize that for many cancer survivors, job discrimination is often worse than fighting the disease. It is estimated that at least one in four survivors of cancer experiences job discrimination. Some research reports the numbers of cancer survivors experiencing job discrimination may be as high as 50 percent (Pardeck, 1994).

Job discrimination is common among cancer survivors because of stereotypes and myths. One common belief is that cancer survivors have high absenteeism from the workplace because of long-term medical problems, but there is no basis to this belief. Many employers and employees have a traditional view of cancer; they simply think cancer equals death. The general population, including employers and employees, do not realize that cancer can be cured or controlled. Cancer survivors can lead long and productive careers. Unfortunately, some employers discriminate against cancer survivors because they simply do not feel comfortable having them in the workplace; there are even some who think cancer is contagious. Given the myths and stereotypes about cancer, survivors of the disease frequently experience discrimination in the workplace. There are more than eight million cancer survivors in the United States; they thus represent a very large minority group that has historically experienced job discrimination (Pardeck, 1996).

The Organizational Setting and a Discrimination Case

This case occurred in a large state agency (Pardeck, 1996). The organization was highly bureaucratic and generally had a history of lacking sensitivity to diversity and human rights. Specific cases of discrimination were reported not only on the basis of disability, but also of race and gender. The organization in one case spent over $150,000 defending a charge of racial discrimination and lost. There were probably other cases of discrimination in the organization that were settled discreetly, unknown to the public. Workers in the agency often described the administrative hierarchy as being stuck in a 1950s mentality toward civil rights. The organization had little tolerance for dissent, and the internal due process mechanism for employees was largely a farce.

A large number of the people in administrative positions achieved their rank in the organization on the basis of nepotism. Given this fact, many of the administrators lacked basic job competencies and had a vested interest in protecting each other's jobs even if civil rights laws (i.e., the ADA) were knowingly violated.

An earlier discrimination case in the organization based on race provided insight into how the organization would react when accused of employment discrimination based on disability. The case involving discrimination on the basis of race became public knowledge through the local newspaper. The media coverage of the case made it obvious that the administrators in the organization would protect each other at almost any cost. It was also clear that the organization had little understanding of civil rights laws. Evident in the news reports concerning the discrimination was that even after the organization settled the case, which cost over $150,000, it did not admit to the discrimination and, more important, made little change in organizational policy to prevent future discrimination (Pardeck, 1996).

James L., the person with a history of cancer, and the focus of the case, applied for a promotion to an administrative position. A number of key administrators were well aware of James L.'s history of cancer. One high-ranking administrator who was not aware of his history asked if he would be interested in the promotion even before the position was advertised publicly. James L. told the administrator he would be interested; however, he stated to the administrator that he left a prior position of similar rank in another state agency because of complications related to the cancer recovery. James L. felt that once this high-ranking administrator found out about his history of cancer, she was no longer interested in promoting him to the position. A fellow employee in the organization told James L. that this high-ranking administrator, after she discovered that he had a history of cancer, asked if he knew James L. was recovering from cancer when the organization hired him (Pardeck, 1996).

The initial strategy used by James L. was to work within the organization. He decided to discuss the discrimination he felt he was experiencing with the human resources officer. The goal of this meeting was to see if the failure to promote James L. could be corrected. Another goal was to explore ways that the organization might be more sensitive to issues related to disabilities and to ensure that the Americans With Disabilities Act was being implemented appropriately. After a discussion with the human resources officer, James L. concluded that the organization was not willing to correct its discriminatory acts against him. It also became clear to him that the internal due process mechanism would prove fruitless.

James L. had always received the highest job performance rankings possible within the organization. As mentioned earlier, he had an informal interview with a high-ranking administrator about the position. Two weeks after this informal interview, James L. officially applied for the promotion. He was not even granted an interview for the position during the search process. Given this situation, he went to the human resources officer about the dynamics that had taken place during the job selection. James L. was assured by the human resources officer that his history of cancer had nothing to do with the failure of the organization to grant him an interview or to promote him to the position. As noted previously, James L. felt the internal system designed to resolve job-related complaints within the organization would not work effectively on his behalf.

A key informant concurred that James L.'s history of cancer probably played a role in his being denied the promotion. The informant, however, did add that James L.'s references from his prior job were distorted by influential people within the organization. This distortion allowed those involved in the selection process to justify their actions of not promoting him. Since James L.'s work record within the organization was excellent, he felt that the distortion of references from his prior job was the organization's strategy to justify its actions. His work history prior to coming to the organization was also excellent.

Since many of the administrators in the organization were hired on the basis of nepotism and not merit, their reaction to James L.'s discussion with the human resources officer was negative and unsophisticated. Prior challenges to the organization based on violations of civil rights law suggested that the agency would spend a great deal of time and resources defending itself even when obvious civil rights violations had occurred.

James L. decided to file a discrimination complaint with the Equal Employment Opportunity Commission under the Americans With Disabilities Act. As noted previously, James L. had discussed his case with the agency's human resources officer and concluded that the agency had no interest in discovering the truth concerning his case. James L. also had little faith in the procedures the agency used for employees who filed grievances against it.

The complaint filed with the EEOC under the Americans With Disabilities Act alleged that James L. was a highly qualified candidate for the administrative position he had applied for within the agency. Not only was he not appointed to the position, the agency even denied him an interview. James L. argued that the agency's discriminatory actions were based on his history of cancer (Pardeck, 1996).

The EEOC's investigation, which took nearly one year, concluded that discrimination had not occurred in James L.'s case. The EEOC claimed the organization's stated nondiscriminatory reason for not granting an interview—a supposedly weak reference from a former employer—was sufficient to find no reasonable cause to believe discrimination occurred based on the investigation's findings.

As James L. had feared, retaliation did occur because of the complaint. Two incidents of harassment occurred, both involving James L.'s immediate supervisor. James L. was called into his supervisor's office; the supervisor then harassed James L. about filing the complaint and said he could not understand "why you want to sue the agency." The second act of retaliation occurred when the supervisor announced during a staff meeting that James L. had filed the complaint. James L. was present at the meeting, and many who attended were not aware of the complaint. James L. consulted with the EEOC about the supervisor's behavior; the EEOC suggested he could file another complaint under the ADA based on retaliation. James L. decided not to do so.

After the EEOC found no merit in James L.'s complaint based on information gathered during its investigation, he received a "right to sue letter." This letter allows a complainant to sue in federal court. Even though the EEOC found no reasonable cause to believe discrimination occurred, James L. still consulted an attorney. The attorney agreed to take his case on a contingency-fee basis. The attorney also suggested that the organization had to spend thousands of dollars defending itself against James L.'s discrimination complaint.

After James L.'s case, the organization appeared to place greater emphasis on the importance of fair hiring and promotion procedures. This was evidenced by memos to employees throughout the organization related to employment discrimination and, in particular, by revisions to the personnel manual. These revisions included new protections for individuals of protected classes in employment, with particular emphasis on protecting people with disabilities from discrimination (Pardeck, 1996).

Legal Proof Scheme Applied to James L.'s Case

Under the ADA, the complainant, James L., had to show he was protected by the ADA. He was able to document this protected status because he had a history of cancer and his employer was aware of this fact.

James L. also had to meet the second step in the proof scheme, that being to show he was qualified for the position. Under the ADA, the complainant must show he or she is a "qualified individual with a disability" with or without reasonable accommodations. James L. was able to show he met the job qualifications.

After James L. was denied an interview for the position, the organization continued to seek out other candidates for the position. Thus another step in the legal proof scheme was met.

The organization had then to give a nondiscriminatory reason for why it failed to promote James L. The reason given, which the EEOC accepted as valid, was a weak job reference. James L. felt that this reference was distorted by the organization because it was from his former employer, who gave him a glowing letter of recommendation for excellent job performance prior to his resigning.

CONCLUSIONS AND IMPLICATIONS

Hopkins and Nestleroth (1991:35) report that Evan J. Kemp, a former chairman of the EEOC and disabilities activist, was once asked why we discriminate against people with disabilities. Kemp answered, "Because some people are terrified of getting old or becoming disabled themselves. They're afraid that knowing people with disabilities in normal settings will make them even more uncomfortable about those possibilities." Given this situation, Kemp concludes that one of the most effective strategies employers can use to change such attitudes of the able is sensitivity training. Even though the ADA does not mandate this kind of training, human services agencies may find it useful because it will increase employee awareness of the unique needs of people with disabilities.

Fersh and Thomas (1993: 129–130) suggest that sensitivity training programs should include information on the new terminology used to describe people with disabilities. Examples are replacing the word "handicapped" with the more neutral terms "disabled" and "disability" and the discarding of phrases such as "suffer from," "victim of," and "crippled by." A person has cancer, for example, and is not afflicted with or suffering from cancer. To many of the 43 million people covered under the ADA, certain phrases and adjectives are inappropriate and demeaning.

Administrators in social work agencies should actively work toward the integration of people with disabilities in the workplace. Practitioners within agencies should also be fully informed of the various components of the ADA because it governs virtually every aspect of agency life. Social workers must realize the intent of the ADA is to mainstream people with disabilities into the workplace as well as the larger society.

As the situational analyses offered earlier imply, there are numerous ways supervisors and employees can violate Title I (the employment provisions) of the ADA if they lack awareness of this law and sensitivity toward people with disabilities. Supervisors and others must also realize they cannot use ignorance of the ADA as a defense against employment discrimination (Pardeck and Chung, 1992).

One of the reasons for the law's creation, as stated in the act (Americans With Disabilities Act P.L. 101–336, 1990: 5), is that "individuals with disabilities are a distinct and insular minority who have been faced with restrictions and limitations and subjected to unequal treatment." As J. P. Shapiro (1993) notes, people with disabilities can be considered the nation's largest minority group, and approximately half of the 43 million Americans with disabilities perceive themselves as a minority. The profession of social work at all levels, including practice and educational settings, must adjust to this new minority group self-image emerging within the disability community. Shapiro's book, *No Pity: People With Disabilities Forging a New Civil Rights Movement* (1993), should be essential reading for all social workers attempting to understand the disabilities civil rights movement leading to the passage of the ADA.

Finally, the changing image of people with disabilities reflected in the definition of a disability under the ADA must be clearly understood by social work supervisors and other employees. As noted in Chapter 2, many of the complaints filed with the EEOC for job discrimination have been by those with hidden disabilities. In fact, the first case (*EEOC v. AIC Security Investigations LTD, 1993*) that resulted in the plaintiff's being awarded over $200,000 involved job discrimination against a cancer patient. Those with a conventional view of disabilities might find it surprising that the first major case won by a plaintiff under the ADA involved this kind of disability; this case confirms the changing image of the meaning of disabilities as a result of the ADA (Bennett-Alexander and Pincus, 1995). Furthermore, those with conventional views of disabilities may not realize that the disabilities rights movement is radically reshaping the world of people with disabilities. The following quotation from Shapiro (1993: 13–14) captures the changes occurring within the disability community: "The 43 million disabled Americans have come to take a growing pride in being identified as disabled. And, like blacks, women, and gays before them, they are challenging the way America looks at them."

REFERENCES

Adaptive Environments Center Inc. (1992). *ADA Title II action guide*. Horsham, PA: Axon Group.

Allen, J. G. (1994). *Successful job search strategies for the disabled: Understanding the ADA*. New York: John Wiley & Sons.

The Americans With Disabilities Act of 1989. (1989). Washington, DC: Government Printing Office.

The Americans With Disabilities Act of 1990. (1990). P. L. 101–336, 105 Stat. 327, 42 U.S.C., 12101 et seq.

Bennett-Alexander, D. L., and Pincus, L. B. (1995). *Employment law for business.* Chicago: Irwin.

EEOC v. AIC Security Investigations LTD. (1993). *BNA'S Americans With Disabilities Act manual (1995).* Washington, DC: The Bureau of National Affairs.

Equal Employment Opportunity Commission and U.S. Department of Justice. (1992). *The Americans With Disabilities Act: Questions and answers.* Washington, DC: National Institute on Disabilities and Rehabilitation Research.

———. (1991). *Americans With Disabilities Act handbook.* Washington, DC: Government Printing Office.

Fersh, D., and Thomas, P. W. (1993). *Complying with the Americans With Disabilities Act.* Westport, CT: Quorum Books.

Great Plains Disability and Business Technical Assistance Center. (1995). *Americans With Disabilities Act technical assistance manual Title II.* Columbia, MO: Great Plains Disability and Business Technical Assistance Center.

Greenlaw, P. S., & Kohl, J. P. (1996). Proving ADA discrimination: The court's view. *Labor Law Journal* 46: 376–383.

Hopkins, K. T., & Nestleroth, S. L. (1991). Willing and able. *Business Week* 28: 35.

Pardeck, J. T. (1996). *Social work practice: An ecological approach.* Westport, CT: Auburn House.

———. (1994, July/August). What you need to know about the Americans With Disabilities Act. *Coping,* 16–17.

Pardeck, J. T., and Chung, W. S. (1992). An analysis of the Americans With Disabilities Act of 1990. *Journal of Health and Social Policy*: 4: 47–56.

Shapiro, J. P. (1993). *No pity: People with disabilities forging a new civil rights movement.* New York: Times Books.

Chapter 5

Education and the Americans With Disabilities Act

The focus of this chapter is the ADA's impact on public and private schools. Professional social workers must realize that Titles II (State and Local Government) and III (Public Accommodations) have explicit requirements concerning the treatment of students with disabilities. One of the purposes of Titles II and III is to integrate students with disabilities into educational settings to the fullest extent possible, and to provide them with the same educational opportunities enjoyed by others.

This chapter discusses the actions schools must take under the ADA to integrate students with disabilities. Also emphasized are the actions barred by the ADA in school settings. Much of this information can be applied to all levels of the educational institutions, from primary through graduate schools. An effort is made to distinguish the differences mandated by the ADA for treating students in public and private educational institutions.

A critical analysis of the ADA in higher education is also presented in this chapter. It is suggested that many of the requirements under the ADA are built on Section 504 of the Rehabilitation Act of 1973. In many ways the ADA does not break new ground in higher education because of its similarity to Section 504. Since little case law has emerged under the ADA in higher education, analyses of Section 504 disability cases are offered; these provide social work educators with critical information concerning the treatment of students with disabilities. The implications of the ADA in the area of admissions is particularly relevant for faculty and administrators in higher education.

The chapter concludes with the topic of ADA educational complaints and enforcement. It is emphasized that public and private schools have different processes for dealing with complaints under ADA. Information is presented concerning the kinds of documentation that is requested by an enforcement agency when a complaint is filed.

ACTIONS EDUCATIONAL INSTITUTIONS MUST TAKE

The ADA guarantees the rights of students with disabilities in educational institutions. The reader should note that there are other disability laws affecting students with disabilities, such an the Individuals With Disabilities Education Act (IDEA). However, IDEA, like other disability laws affecting educational institutions, is narrow in its coverage. The ADA is not; it affects every aspect of the educational environment.

The ADA has four basic standards that govern the treatment of students with disabilities (Morrissey, 1993):

1. The program, service, or activity, when viewed in its entirety, must be readily accessible to and usable by people with disabilities.

2. A person with a disability must be able to access and act on information about a program, service, or activity.

3. When evaluating students with disabilities, screening and testing procedures must be fair, accurate, and nondiscriminatory.

4. Students with disabilities must be able to participate in an activity, service, or program offered to other students.

The ADA does not provide educators with a simple set of requirements; they are complex. ADA cases in an educational setting must be judged on a case-by-case basis. However, there are a number of clear requirements that educational institutions must follow under the ADA.

Integration and Accessibility

Educational institutions must ensure that programs are offered in the most integrated setting for students with disabilities. This is possible only if the program and facility housing the program are accessible to students with disabilities.

Integration is mandated by the ADA even if modifications are needed to a program so a student with a disability can participate. If a modification to the program is not possible, a school must offer separate opportunities for the student; however, this approach is a strategy of last resort. Under Title II, as mentioned earlier, if an entity offers a separate program, including an educational program, the person with a disability can decline to participate in favor of the integrated program.

Program Accessibility

Integrating students with disabilities can require modifications in program policies, practices, and procedures. The ADA requires educational institutions to make reasonable modifications to a program as long as they do not fundamentally alter the program or result in undue financial or administrative hardship (Morrissey, 1993). Reasonable modifications include the following:

1. Notifying potential students that a range of services and programs is available to students with disabilities, including filling out forms and obtaining modified textbooks, and telling them where to call for information.

2. Offering returning students with disabilities a chance to register for classes early so any special adjustments they need can be arranged before school or classes start.

3. Letting a student with disabilities take an exam at a different time or place than other students.

4. If a student with disabilities transfers to the school during the academic year, reassigning a class to a different room if the student can not reach the original room because of his or her disability.

5. Letting students with certain kinds of disabilities (for example, mobility impairments) leave their final class early so they can safely board buses before the rush of other students.

6. Training faculty members about the types of modifications they can make to accommodate students with disabilities.

These are examples of modifications that would fundamentally alter an educational program (Morrissey, 1993):

1. Waiving an entrance requirement to a course or activity when the requirement bears directly on the student's chance of success.

2. Putting a student with a disability in a class in which he or she would require so much individual attention from the teacher that it would substantially reduce the amount of instruction offered to other students.

3. Placing a student with disabilities in a class in which auxiliary aids that he or she needs or behavior that the student exhibits would substantially affect other students' ability to learn.

Educators have a right to expect students with disabilities to take exams and complete course requirements. At the same time, however, educators should recognize that under the ADA they can rarely justify excluding a student with a disability from a class or program. In most cases, reasonable modifications can be made so they can participate (Morrissey, 1993).

Physical Accessibility

Even though the requirements for physical accessibility are not specified in the ADA, at least one standard is suggested (Morrissey, 1993). For example, college students with disabilities should have access to at least one biology lab, but not all of the labs. Furthermore, there should be at least one location accessible to all services on campus.

Carrying a student up or down stairs is not considered a method of achieving physical accessibility to a program. Carrying a student is permitted only in manifestly exceptional circumstances, and is not an alternative to installing a ramp or chair lift. In cases where carrying is the only option, the persons carrying the student with a disability must have received formal training on the safest and least humiliating method (Morrissey, 1993).

What constitutes a reasonable modification for a public school may be considered unreasonable for a private school. According to the ADA, there are three fundamental differences between the obligations of public and private schools (Morrissey, 1993):

1. Public schools normally have the option of moving a classroom from one floor to another or offering a service at alternative locations. Private schools, on the other hand, often must work within the constraints of a single site.

2. For a public system, a shift in location or removing barriers to services does not necessarily represent an additional cost. For a private educational system, such actions may cost additional money.

3. Ensuring physical access often requires removing a barrier or offering alternatives to barrier removal. The degree of such modifications required of private schools must be reasonable, inexpensive, and easy to implement. Public schools, on the other hand, must make such modifications unless doing so would create an undue financial or administrative hardship.

One other important difference between public and private schools under the ADA affects cases in which an official denies access to a student with a disability because the modification would fundamentally alter a program or result in undue hardship. Public school officials who make this decision must put it in writing and sign it. There is no such requirements of an official in a private school (Morrissey, 1993).

Safety

Schools, both public and private, can impose requirements aimed at protecting students' safety. Such requirements, however, cannot be based on fears, stereotypes, or assumptions about students with disabilities. The following are examples of safety requirements involving students with disabilities (Morrissey, 1993):

1. A student with cerebral palsy should be allowed to participate on a swim team if he or she can perform the required swimming strokes and qualifies for the team. How the student gets to the side of the pool or into and out of it may involve help from others, but this cannot be the basis for excluding the student from the swim team.

2. A student with a disability associated with high levels of fatigue may not be able to safely take a six-hour bus ride on a field trip. Students with other kinds of disabilities, for example, an emotional impairment or learning disability, usually do not pose safety risks with or without assistance or supervision.

3. Most students with disabilities in primary grades cannot be denied access to the playground because of safety concerns.

Communication With Students With Disabilities

The communication requirements for students with disabilities under the ADA are clear. These requirements include simple actions, such as writing a brief message on a note pad for a deaf student, to more complex actions, such as providing a reader for a student who is blind.

There are two limits on what educational institutions must do in the area of communication for students with disabilities. One, schools are not required to do anything that would fundamentally alter a program or result in financial or administrative hardship. Second, schools do not have to make the latest or most expensive assistive technology available to students with disabilities. The following are the general requirements concerning communication under the ADA (Morrissey, 1993):

1. Schools should give primary consideration to the preference of students with a disability in choosing which type of auxiliary aid or service to provide.

2. Telecommunication devices should be installed for the deaf or hearing-impaired so that the school can communicate effectively with these students.

3. Schools must ensure that students with disabilities, including those with vision and hearing impairments, are able to get information about the availability of accessible services and facilities.

4. The international symbol for accessibility should be posted at the entrance of every school building that is accessible.

Last, it must be noted that when schools recruit students, the ADA mandates that individuals with disabilities have the same opportunity as others to information about educational programs.

Testing Procedure

The ADA has a number of requirements that affect the testing process. The following are the general requirements that schools must follow in testing students with disabilities who need accommodation (Morrissey, 1993):

1. A student may need to have additional time to take a test.

2. The test may have to be read to the student.

3. A student may have to take the test at a different time or place than others.

4. The student may have to receive individual proctoring during the test.

5. The student may have to use some other means to demonstrate knowledge or ability that may not be reflected in a standard test.

As indicated in this section, there are limits to the actions schools must take to accommodate students with disabilities. A general requirement under the ADA is that schools do not have to do anything that would fundamentally alter a program or service or cause an undue administrative or financial hardship for them. However, the ADA does mandate that students with disabilities be integrated into classes and activities with able students whenever possible. In most cases, it will be much easier to accommodate students with disabilities than to explain legally why they were denied access to a program or school activity (Morrissey, 1993).

ACTIONS BARRED BY THE ADA

The previous section focused on what educational institutions must do; this part focuses on what schools cannot do. The reader will find that much of what schools cannot do is simply the opposite of what they must do. In many cases, the actions barred by the ADA are also prohibited under Section 504 of the Rehabilitation Act of 1973.

Educational institutions cannot do anything that discriminates against persons with disabilities. There are only a few limited circumstances in which denying access to a program or service is permitted under the ADA. It is much easier for schools not to discriminate than to later face a legal challenge. Keeping this point in mind, the following actions are barred under the ADA for both public and private educational systems (Morrissey, 1993).

Generalizations

Every decision that affects a person with a disability must be made on a case-by-case basis. For example, a rule that states that all visually impaired students are barred from a program is probably a violation of the ADA.

Denial of Opportunity

A school cannot deny a qualified student with a disability the opportunity to participate in or to benefit from programs or activities offered by a school system.

Unequal Opportunity

Educational institutions cannot offer lesser opportunities to students with disabilities than are offered to others. For example, a student with a disability has the same right to eat in a school cafeteria as do able students.

Separate or Different Opportunities

A school cannot provide a different or separate opportunity unless it can be determined that this modification is truly necessary. Schools must also determine if the adjustment can be provided in an integrated environment.

Right to Decline Separate or Different Programs

Schools cannot deny students with disabilities the opportunity to participate in services or programs with able students, even if separate or different programs are available. Thus, schools cannot require qualified students with disabilities to take separate gym or other classes. This mandate enforces integration and choice for students with disabilities.

Right to Decline Special Aids or Services

Students with disabilities have the right to decline special aids and services they are offered by a school. For example, they can decline a special seat, equipment, or help offered by the school.

Use of Discriminatory Criteria

Educational institutions cannot use criteria or methods of administration that discriminate against persons with disabilities. For example, under the ADA a teacher cannot require that all assignments be in writing. A student with a disability may have to demonstrate knowledge of a topic in a different format because of his or her disability.

Discrimination Through Eligibility Criteria

Educational institutions cannot impose eligibility criteria that tend to screen out students with disabilities from programs or services. An exception to this requirement is allowed if the criteria are essential to the program or services.

Surcharges

Students with disabilities cannot be charged for an accommodation. For example, if a student needs an interpreter as an accommodation, the school cannot charge the student for this service.

Discrimination Through Association

Educational institutions cannot discriminate against a person because he or she has a relationship with a person with a disability. For example, a student cannot be denied admission to a sporting event because he or she is accompanied by a friend who has an emotional impairment.

Retaliation

Educational institutions cannot take a negative action against an individual because he or she opposed a practice made unlawful by the ADA. This requirement protects both persons with disabilities and the nondisabled who file complaints under the ADA.

Coercion

Schools cannot coerce, intimidate, threaten, or interfere with any individual who exercises his or her rights under the ADA. This companion requirement to retaliation covers both persons with disabilities and those involved in exercising another's rights under the ADA.

ANALYSIS OF THE AMERICANS WITH DISABILITIES ACT IN HIGHER EDUCATION

As mentioned previously, the Americans With Disabilities Act is built on Section 504 of the Rehabilitation Act of 1973. Even though the ADA does not break new ground for higher education, it confirms and consolidates gains made in previous disabilities legislation and case law. Section 504 provided initial coverage designed to redress discrimination against persons with disabilities in colleges and universities receiving federal funding. The regulations of Section 504 have been in effect for all social work programs receiving federal funding since the 1970s (Cole, Christ, and Light, 1995).

Section 504 of the Rehabilitation Act of 1973

The purpose of Section 504 is to ensure that persons with disabilities will not be discriminated against by any recipient of federal funding: "No otherwise qualified individual with a handicap . . . shall, solely by reason of her or his handicap, be excluded from participation in . . . any program or activity receiving federal financial assistance" (Section 504 Title VI of the Rehabilitation Act of 1973). Section 504, is patterned after Title VI of the Civil Rights Act of 1964, which prohibits sex and race discrimination in federally funded programs and activities.

A complainant filing a charge under Section 504 must establish four conditions. First, a complainant must have a handicap, which is defined as (1) a physical or mental impairment that substantially limits one or more major life activities; (2) a record of such an impairment; or (3) being regarded as having an impairment. Second, the complainant must be "otherwise qualified" (Department of Education Regulations, 1980), which has been described by one court ruling (*Southeastern Community College v. Davis*, 1979) as a person who meets programmatic requirements in spite of the disability. Section 504 further defines "otherwise qualified" to include one who with a "reasonable accommodation can perform the essential functions" of the activity in question (Department of Education Regulations, 1980). Educational institutions are not required to make fundamental changes to existing programs that would impose an undue hardship on the institution to accommodate an otherwise qualified student. However, if a post-secondary program fails to make a reasonable accommodation, as established though a determination of the facts, this failure does constitute discrimination (Department of Education Regulations, 1980). Third, the educational institution must receive federal funds. Finally, the complainant must establish that the denial of access or benefit was due to the person's disability.

For academic programs, academic requirements that are viewed as essential to the program will not have to be modified to meet the needs of a student with disabilities. Examples of appropriate modifications that educational programs may have to make include adapting course methods, supplying auxiliary aids for students in class, and altering examination methods.

The Americans With Disabilities Act

The ADA resembles Section 504, but greatly expands protection against discrimination in numerous areas, including employment in public and private settings (Title I); activities of state and local government, including public educational institutions (Title II); services offered by private entities including private schools (Title III); and telecommunications services (Title IV).

Of particular interest to post-secondary institutions is the fact that retaliation against, interference with, or intimidation of a person who exercises his or her rights under the ADA is forbidden. Furthermore, the court may award attorney's fees and other compensatory damages to a prevailing plaintiff. Finally, Title V of the ADA defines the following personal characteristics not to be disabilities under the act: homosexuality, bisexuality, transvestitism, transsexualism, pedophilia, exhibitionism, voyeurism, compulsive gambling, kleptomania, pyromania, and psychoactive substance use.

Comparison of Section 504 and the Americans With Disabilities Act

Colleges and universities must follow the regulations of Section 504 if they receive federal funds. The ADA simply extends coverage and protection for persons with disabilities in some areas, particularly for private employers. Within the post-secondary setting, the ADA has far-reaching effects because it applies not merely to the educational programs for students, but to all services offered to the public sector. Numerous cases decided under Section 504 define and interpret the terms used in the ADA's prohibition of discrimination. The ADA codifies much of Section 504's case law and incorporates much of its language. Section 504 and the ADA both define a disability, a qualified person with a disability, and a reasonable accommodation.

What Is a Disability?

The ADA and Section 504 use the same definition of a person with a disability. An individual is defined as having a disability if he or she: (1) has a physical or mental impairment that substantially limits one or more major life activities; (2) has a record of such an impairment; and (3) is regarded as having an impairment.

Based on the case law and committee reports interpreting Section 504, Congress added to Section 504's illustrations of qualifying conditions "contagious and noncontagious" diseases as qualifying disabilities under the ADA's Test 1. These diseases include HIV and tuberculosis. Excluded by the ADA are gender identity disorders, sexual behavior disorders, and psychoactive substance-use disorders.

Who Is a Qualified Individual?

The ADA protects qualified individuals with a disability from discrimination. A qualified individual is defined as a disabled individual who meets the essential eligibility requirements for a program, activity, or job (Raines and Rossow, 1994). There are two steps used to determine if a person is qualified under the ADA. First, the person must meet the prerequisites of the program, job, or activity; second, it must be determined whether the individual can perform the essential functions necessary, with or without a reasonable accommodation.

In determining whether a student with a disability is qualified under both the ADA and Section 504, the following factors are considered. First, does the student meet the basic prerequisites for admission to an academic or professional program? Second, can reasonable accommodations be made for the student that will allow him or her to be admitted? If a student's disability becomes an issue after admission to an educational program, the same standards for reasonable accommodations are applied for retention.

What Is a Reasonable Accommodation?

Once an academic program has been notified that a student has a disability, the program must provide reasonable accommodations that allow the student access to facilities and services. A reasonable accommodation is any change made in the program that will result in equal opportunity or access for a person with a disability. These include removing architectural barriers, providing interpreters, acquiring special equipment, or changing educational policies. What is reasonable in one individual's case may not be reasonable in another's, so a case-by-case determination must be made by the academic program.

Neither Section 504 nor the ADA requires an accommodation to be made if it imposes an undue hardship; this determination is also made on an ad hoc basis. The standard for proving undue hardship is more stringent under the ADA than under Section 504 because the ADA requires that expenses for an accommodation be determined by the size, financial resources, nature, and structure of the program or facility. Section 504 defines an undue hardship more generally, basing it on a department's budget and operation, and on the nature and cost of the accommodation (Pardeck and Chung, 1992).

ANALYSIS OF LITIGATION

There have been numerous court rulings under Section 504; the case law that has developed from these rulings is the best guide for understanding the requirements of the ADA for social work programs. These rulings deal with the definition of disability, of a qualified person with a disability, and of what are reasonable accommodations. Even though none of these rulings is related directly to social work programs, they still have important implications for social work educators.

Definition of a Disability

The most frequently cited case for determining whether a condition qualifies as a disability is *School Board of Nassau County v. Arline* (1987). In this case, the court held that a teacher with tuberculosis was protected under Section 504, even though contagious diseases previously were not considered a disability. The court ruled that to allow discrimination on the basis of a contagious disease is inconsistent with the purpose of Section 504—to ensure that persons are not discriminated against because of the prejudice or ignorance of others.

A second case, *Nathanson v. Medical College of Pennsylvania* (1991), addressed the question of who bears responsibility for informing authorities about a disabling condition and when this should occur during the student's education. A former medical student sued an institution for not providing special accommodations in the form of seating and parking arrangements to accommodate her spasmodically painful back and neck injuries. When the student was admitted to the medical program, she indicated on her application that she had prior injuries that would require special accommodations. She requested and received special seating accommodations when she took her Medical College Admissions Tests. During the first week of class she aggravated her back condition and requested an accommodation for seating. The school did not meet her request and encouraged her to take a leave of absence until her back improved. Even though the court ruled in favor of the university, the court noted that institutional responsibility hinges on whether the college knows of or could reasonably be expected to know of the student's disability and the need for accommodation.

Issues of Qualification and Reasonable Accommodation

Over the past several years, the courts have broadened their interpretation of "otherwise qualified" to include consideration of what reasonable accommodations could be made to assist a student with a disability.

The 1979 ruling in *Southeastern Community College v. Davis* (1980) addressed the obligations imposed under Section 504 on a nursing program to admit a nearly deaf student. The prospective nursing student, who relied on lip-reading in addition to her hearing aid, was denied admission to a nursing program. The Supreme Court upheld the denial by ruling that an otherwise qualified individual is one who is able to meet all requirements in spite of his or her handicap. Furthermore, the Supreme Court concluded that to require the program to make substantial adjustments beyond those illuminating discrimination would be an unauthorized extension of the obligations of Section 504. In essence, Section 504 imposes no requirement on an educational institution to lower or make substantial modifications of its standards to accommodate a person with a disability. An important implication of the ruling was that the issue of "otherwise qualified" was separate from and had to be addressed before the question of whether the program needs to make a reasonable accommodation for a student.

The *Southeastern Community College v. Davis* ruling was applied and modified in the *Kling v. County of Los Angeles* (1980) case. In this case an applicant with Crohn's disease sought admission to a nursing education program. The school did not argue that the student was not qualified, but that the student would probably miss too many classes and was therefore denied admission. The court ruled that the program had to admit the student and accommodate her need for remedial instruction. The case was later overturned on a procedural issue.

The Supreme Court moderated the *Southeastern Community College v. Davis* ruling in *Alexander v. Choate* (1985). The *Davis* ruling concluded that students first needed to be qualified for a program before considering the question of whether to provide reasonable accommodations. The court concluded in *Alexander v. Choate*:

> The balance struck in Davis requires that an otherwise qualified handicapped individual must be provided with meaningful access to the benefit that the grantee offers. The benefit itself, of course, cannot be defined in a way that effectively denies otherwise qualified handicapped individuals the meaningful access to which they are entitled; to assure meaningful access, reasonable accommodations in the grantee's program or benefit may have to be made. (p. 301)

Two years later, in the *School Board of Nassau County v. Arline* (1987), the Supreme Court decision appeared to blend the troublesome relationship between "otherwise qualified" and "reasonable accommodation." The Supreme Court ruled that when a disabled person is not able to perform the essential functions of the job, the court must also consider whether any reasonable accommodation by the employer would permit the disabled person to perform those functions.

In *Wynne v. Tufts University School of Medicine* (1991), a student diagnosed as having cognitive deficits and weakness in processing discrete units of information failed a required course for the second time and requested that the program alter its format of testing. The school countered that the student, who was not identified as disabled at the time of admission, could not be an otherwise qualified individual eligible for a reasonable accommodation because he had failed eight of fifteen courses during his first year of the program. The court ruled that the school met its burden of proving that it had considered alternatives and that no further accommodation could be made without imposing an undue hardship on the academic program.

In *Pushkin v. Regents of the University of Colorado* (1981), the court concluded that a physician suffering from multiple sclerosis was otherwise qualified and had been wrongfully denied admission to the university's psychiatric residency training program. In a related case, *Doe v. New York University* (1981), the court ruled, however, that a medical program had a legal right to deny readmission of a student after recurrence of her borderline personality disorder. The institution based its finding on the significant risk of recurrence of the disorder and the potential risk the student posed to patients.

Doherty v. Southern College of Optometry (1987) illustrates the problem of balancing the requirements of "otherwise qualified" and "reasonable accommodation." In this case the court found that a college could refuse to waive clinical proficiency requirements for an admitted student with retinitis pigmentosoa and an undiagnosed neurological condition. The court ruled that the student was not otherwise qualified for an optometry degree when he could not pass a mandatory clinical proficiency examination. The program was not required to make any accommodation that would result in a substantial change to or lowering of a program's requirements.

In a case involving dismissal of a dental student (*Doe v. Washington University*, 1991) who had tested positive for HIV, the dental program prevailed. The school argued that the student was not otherwise qualified because of the significant probability of the student's transmitting the disease to patients. The court accepted the university's decision to dismiss the student.

"Otherwise qualified" and "reasonable accommodation" are closely intertwined. Determination of whether a student is otherwise qualified depends in part on the reasonableness of the accommodation required. Social work programs need not lower or change academic standards to accommodate students. If a school determines that an accommodation is not reasonable, it must be able to document by professional and academic judgment that no reasonable alternative exists that would meet both the goals of the program and the needs of the student.

Implications of ADA Policy for Social Work Programs

The Americans With Disabilities Act is clearly grounded in the human rights perspective. The ADA, like other civil rights legislation of the past, is aimed at an oppressed group that has been denied equal opportunity to participate in society.

It is significant that under the ADA, persons with disabilities are defined as a minority group. This definition suggests, for example, that if the disabled person is poor, it is less a result of personal inadequacy than of a discriminatory society. Consequently, the adjustment to a disability is not merely a personal problem but one requiring the adjustment of the larger society to the person with disabilities. This position requires that society adjust its attitudes and, as such, remove the obstacles it has placed in the way of self-fulfillment for people with disabilities (Karger and Stoesz, 1994). This orientation has great importance for social work programs.

The research also suggests that, like other oppressed groups, people with disabilities have suffered tremendous discrimination. Two reports by The National Council on Disability titled "Toward Independence" (1986) and "On the Threshold of Independence" (1988), a study titled "Accommodating the Spectrum of Individual Abilities" (1983) by the Civil Rights Commission, and national polls have all concluded that discrimination against people with disabilities is pervasive in American society (Pardeck and Chung, 1992). This discrimination is sometimes a result of prejudice or patronizing attitudes, and still other times it is the result of indifference or thoughtlessness. Whatever the origin, the outcomes are the same: exclusion, segregation, and the denial of equal, effective, and meaningful opportunities to participate in activities and programs. The ADA is aimed at preventing and correcting the numerous problems associated with discrimination against people with disabilities (Pardeck and Chung, 1992).

The ADA has important implications for social work programs particularly in the area of admission and retention of students with disabilities. Since the ADA is a new law, Section 504 provides the most useful guide to the rights and responsibilities of social work faculty under the ADA.

Three questions should guide the admissions process of social work programs when students with disabilities apply. First, does the student have a disability as defined under the ADA? It must be noted that some students do not wish to declare their disability during the admissions process. If such is the case, the student is not protected by the ADA. Second, will the student be able to meet the competency requirements of social work? Problems of competence emerge when deciding if an applicant, despite the disability, is otherwise qualified to perform the requisite professional skills critical to social work. Third, can the program provide accommodations for the student without imposing an undue hardship on itself? What is important about the issue of accommodations is that each case must be assessed on its own merits. For example, a blanket policy by an admissions committee that states "no applicant will be admitted to the program with a history of emotional disability" is a violation of the ADA. If a student declares a history of a disability, the committee must decide if that disability will prevent the applicant from effectively performing the requisite professional skills critical to social work.

Admissions committees must be certain not to have application forms that directly inquire about the existence of a disability. The application form may, however, request information about the student's abilities to perform specific, essential tasks of social work. It is critical that the admissions committee has a consensus on what the essential tasks of social work consist of and if any of these might be met by students through accommodations.

When an applicant declares a disability that is protected under the ADA, the admissions committee must complete a two-step analysis. First, the committee must determine if the candidate is otherwise qualified. Specifically, can the applicant perform the essential tasks of social work? Second, can a reasonable accommodation be made to enable the prospective student to become a social worker? The committee must make each decision on a case-by-case basis because no two disabilities are alike.

Scott (1994) provides a list of requirements that will help social work faculty decide if an accommodation is reasonable. An accommodation is reasonable if it:

1. Is based on documented individual needs.

2. Allows the most integrated experience possible.

3. Does not compromise the essential requirements of a course or program.

4. Does not pose a threat to personal or public safety.

5. Does not impose undue financial or administrative burden.

If any of the above conditions are not met, it can be concluded that an accommodation is not reasonable.

If the admissions committee decides not to admit the student because the disability is too severe, the applicant may be denied admission (*Southeastern Community College v. Davis*, 1979). However, in *Pushkin v. Regents of the University of Colorado* (1981), a case involving a student with multiple sclerosis applying for a residency program, the court ruled that the applicant could be accommodated even though the school disagreed. The *Kling v. County of Los Angeles* (1980) case suggests that social work programs should not assume a student will miss an extreme amount of course work because of a disability.

Decisions to retain or dismiss a student with disabilities must also be considered by social work programs. If a student is dismissed, the program must be sure the action is not discriminatory. The analysis is similar to that required at admission. The questions that must be answered include: Is the disability so severe that the student cannot do the requisite skills of social work? Can the student's disability be accommodated without altering the standards for skills required of a social worker? The *Doherty v. Southern College of Optometry* (1987) suggests that a social work program can dismiss a student with a disability, without violating the ADA, if it can clearly document that the student cannot master course skills. *Doe v. New York University* (1981), a case in which a student was denied readmission to a medical program, and *Doe v. Washington University* (1981), a ruling involving a student dismissed from dental school because of his disability, suggest that if a student's disability poses a threat to client safety, the student can be dismissed from a social work program.

The statutory language of Section 504 provides guidance for making admission decisions that do not violate the ADA. Even though case law provides guidance for admissions committees, there are many uncertainties that committees must deal with. What admissions committees can clearly anticipate, however, is that students with disabilities will continue to seek careers in social work and that they will continue to challenge decisions that appear to violate their rights under the ADA. Given this situation, it is critical that social work faculty be exposed to the requirements of the ADA. Knowledge of these requirements will help minimize the risks of liability.

COMPLAINTS AND ENFORCEMENT

As this chapter has made clear, the ADA is the broadest based statute guaranteeing the rights of individuals with disabilities. Even though the ADA is a complex law and has a far-reaching scope that affects most of American society, the complaint procedures are relatively simple to implement. These procedures build on Section 504 of the Rehabilitation Act; they are also similar to those found under Title VI of the Civil Rights Act of 1964. Educators who are familiar with the complaint procedures under Section 504 can expect the same procedures under the ADA.

Educational institutions have strong incentives to comply with the ADA because losing a complaint can be extremely costly. Public educational institutions can lose their federal funding if found in violation. Private institutions can be required to pay damages and federal fines up to $50,000 for the first offense and $100,000 for subsequent offenses. Also, public and private educational institutions that lose in court have to pay all attorneys' fees (Morrissey, 1993). It is also important to note that students with disabilities who feel their rights have been violated under the ADA do not have to initiate or complete a local administrative proceeding before going to federal court. This is true for both public and private schools.

Public Institutions

Complaints can be filed by an individual who believes he or she has been discriminated against because of disability, or by his or her authorized representative. Complaints may be filed with any federal agency, all of which must be forwarded to the U.S. Department of Education's Office of Civil Rights for investigation. A complaint must be submitted within 180 days of the alleged discrimination unless the Department of Education extends the deadline. Once a complaint is received, the Department of Education investigates and attempts to resolve the issue informally. If the informal attempt fails, the department will issue a "Letter of Findings" that includes (Morrissey, 1993):

1. Findings of fact and conclusions related to the ADA.

2. A description of what the educational institution must do to resolve each of the violations found.

3. A notice of rights available to the complainant, including the right to sue in court.

The Department of Education will also notify the Department of Justice and embark on formal negotiations with the educational institution to try to achieve voluntary compliance. At this stage, any voluntary compliance that is agreed to must (Morrissey, 1993):

1. Be in writing and signed by both parties.

2. Address each violation.

3. Specify the corrective or remedial action to be taken and a timetable for completion.

4. Provide assurances that the discrimination will not recur.

5. Provide for the enforcement of the agreement by the attorney general.

Last, if voluntary compliance efforts fail, the Department of Education must refer the matter to the attorney general with a recommendation for appropriate action. Such action can include filing a lawsuit in federal court and result in the termination of federal funds to the institution after an administrative hearing (Morrissey, 1993).

Private Institutions

An individual with a disability can proceed against a private institution if she believes she has been discriminated against, or if she has reasonable grounds to believe that she is about to be discriminated against. For example, the person might believe that blueprints or floor plans for alterations or new construction discriminate because they do not provide proper access (Morrissey, 1993).

In either circumstance, the person can file a civil suit seeking preventive relief such as a temporary or permanent injunction or restraining order. If the individual filing suit requests it, the court can appoint an attorney to represent her. In addition, the court can permit the attorney general to intervene in the civil suit if the attorney general certifies that the case is of importance to the general public (Morrissey, 1993).

The court can order a wide range of injunctive relief if it finds the private educational institution guilty of discrimination. The court can require the institution to (Morrissey, 1993):

1. Alter facilities to make them readily accessible to and usable by people with disabilities.

2. Provide that the institution must offer a service or modify a policy.

3. Order the educational institution to provide alternative methods for the person with a disability to complete a task.

The court can also impose fines of up to $50,000 for the first offense and $100,000 for each subsequent offense and require the payment of damages.

Last, the person with a disability can also ask that the attorney general investigate the alleged discrimination.

If a complaint is filed by a person with a disability against a public or private educational institution, school officials should be able to document the following (Morrissey, 1993):

1. All students, including the complainant, are judged on the same standards.

2. All students with the same qualifications and students with the same educational needs and interests are offered the same educational opportunities.

3. If the need for accommodation arose, the staff discussed options with the complainant.

4. The school officials offered reasonable and effective options to the complainant.

If these steps can be documented, the educational institution should be in a strong position to defend any complaint. In terms of organizational behavior, this means that all students should be provided the same educational opportunities regardless of disability and that the institution can document that it has done so.

CONCLUSIONS

This chapter reviews the requirements of public and private educational institutions under the ADA. Most of these requirements concerning the rights of students with disabilities are mandated under Titles II and III of the ADA. The goal of these titles is the integration of students with disabilities into educational programs and services to the fullest extent possible.

As noted in the chapter, Section 504 of the Rehabilitation Act of 1973 and the ADA place similar demands on educational institutions affected by both of these laws. If an institution is in compliance with Section 504, it probably has met most of the mandates under the ADA.

One of the critical issues in the chapter focused on the admissions process used by social work programs to screen applicants for social work education. A number of suggestions were made that may help faculty and social work programs meet the requirements for compliance under the ADA.

Last, the complaint procedures were offered under the ADA for students with disabilities. The differences between the procedures used for public and private educational institutions were covered. It should be clear from the procedures used to investigate complaints by federal agencies that if an educational institution can document that it has offered equal opportunity to students with disabilities, defending complaints becomes an easier task.

REFERENCES

Accommodating the Spectrum of Individual Abilities (1983). *Civil Rights Commission*. Washington, DC: Civil Rights Commission.

Alexander v. Choate, 469 U.S. 287 (1985).

Cole, B. S., Christ, C. C., and Light, T. R. (1995). Social work education and students with disabilities: Implications of Section 504 and the ADA. *Journal of Social Work Education* 31: 261–268.

Department of Education Regulations. (1980), 34 C.F.R. 104 et seq.

Doe v. New York University, 666 F.2d 761 (2nd Cir. 1981).

Doe v. Washington University, 780 F. Supp. 628 (E.D.Mo. 1991).

Doherty v. Southern College of Optometry, 659 F. Supp. 662 (W.D. Tenn. 1987).

Karger, H. J., and Stoesz, D. (1994). *American social welfare: A pluralist approach* (2nd edn.). White Plains, NY: Longman.

Kling v. County of Los Angeles, 633 F. 2d 876 (9th Cir. 1980), 474 U.S. 936 (1985).

Morrissey, P. A. (1993). *The educator's guide to the Americans With Disabilities Act*. Alexandria, VA: American Vocational Association.

Nathanson v. Medical College of Pennsylvania, 926 F.2d 1368 (3rd Cir. 1991).

On the Threshold of Independence (1988). *The National Council on Disability*. Washington, DC: The National Council on Disability.

Pardeck, J. T., & Chung, W. S. (1992). An analysis of the Americans With Disabilities Act of 1990. *Journal of Health and Social Policy*, 4: 47–56.

Pushkin v. Regents of the University of Colorado, 658 F.2d 1372 (10th Cir. 1981).

Raines, J. B., and Rossow, L. F. (1994). The Americans With Disabilities Act: Resolving the separate-but-equal problem in colleges and universities. *West's Education Law Reporter* 88: 1–11.

School Board of Nassau County v. Arline, 480 U.S. 273 (1987).

Scott, S. S. (1994). Determining reasonable academic adjustments for college students with learning disabilities. *Journal of Learning Disabilities* 27: 403–413.

Section 504 Title VI of the Rehabilitation Act of 1973, as amended in 1974 29 U.S.C.A. 794.

Southeastern Community College v. Davis, 442 U.S. 397, 99 S.Ct. 2361 (1979).

Toward Independence (1986). *The National Council on Disability*. Washington, DC: The National Council on Disability.

Wynne v. Tufts University School of Medicine, 932 f.2d 191 (1st Cir. 1991), 976 F. 2d 791 (1st Cir. 1992).

Chapter 6

Advocacy and the Americans With Disabilities Act

A psychosocial perspective views persons with disabilities as being a distinct insular minority group (*Federal Register*, 1980). If a person with a disability is poor, it is less a result of personal inadequacy than of a discriminatory society. A psychosocial model situates the problem of disability in the transaction and interaction of the person with a disability and the social environment. This approach suggests that a disability is not simply a personal problem, but one that requires adjustment of the larger society to people with disabilities (Brothwell and Sandison, 1967; Burgdorf and Burgdorf, 1977). It means that society must change its attitudes and that it must remove the barriers that have been placed in the way of self-fulfillment for people with disabilities. Changing attitudes toward persons with disabilities and their integration into all aspects of society is a core goal of the ADA (Karger and Stoesz, 1994).

Even though disabilities vary greatly among persons, all people with disabilities share one central experience, that being discrimination and oppression. Like other minority groups, persons with disabilities experience poverty and destitution in numbers proportionately larger than the general population (Fiedler, 1978). Persons with disabilities, when compared to able people, tend to more frequently be unemployed or underemployed (Ianacone, 1977). The problems of unemployment and low wages are exacerbated among people with disabilities because they have more frequent need of medical and hospital care than others. Persons with disabilities spend three times more of their own money on medical care than do able bodied people; they also are less likely to have health insurance (Karger and Stoesz, 1994).

People with disabilities now have many new rights and opportunities under the ADA. Even though the ADA has brought about many positive changes for persons with disabilities, much still needs to be done to ensure their integration into society (Pardeck and Chung, 1992). A basic social work strategy such as advocacy, can be an effective approach to ensuring that the ADA is implemented appropriately.

ADVOCACY AND THE AMERICANS WITH DISABILITIES ACT

The goals of advocacy are to achieve social justice and to empower people. Advocacy helps people correct unjust situations. Achieving social justice through advocacy requires the active participation of citizens who are vulnerable or disenfranchised; the professional social worker also plays a critical role in this process. The banding together of those who wish to achieve social justice provides the opportunity for empowerment, for active, responsible participation in the public realm (Lewis, 1992). The role of the advocate is to speak on behalf of clients and to empower clients to speak out when their rights have been denied. The advocacy role is a critical strategy for those who are grounded in a social justice approach to practice because it expands opportunities by protecting the interests of clients. Furthermore, advocacy is a classic role aimed at changing the oppressive social environments of clients, including the various systems that prevent individual growth and development (Pardeck, 1996).

McGowan (1987) concludes that advocacy can be conducted at two levels, case advocacy and cause advocacy. The case advocacy approach focuses on individual cases. It involves partisan intervention on behalf of a client or identified client group with one or more secondary institutions to secure or enhance needed services, resources, or entitlements (McGowan, 1987). Cause advocacy seeks to redress collective issues through social change and improving social policies.

Rees (1991) argues that case and cause advocacy both begin by identifying the dynamics causing social injustice. Rees makes the following conclusion about the advocacy process:

The decision to pursue the advocacy of a case or a cause, or a combination of both, will usually have been preceded by the identification of an injustice which it is felt cannot be rectified simply by efficient administration or negotiation. The identification of an injustice and the sense of conviction concerning the removal of this injustice should become a priority. . . . It is not sufficient merely to recognize an injustice. You have to believe that this issue should be fought for, and if necessary over a long period of time. (p. 146)

The effective advocacy role involves data collection, effective communication with the public through the media, raising revenue, and building coalitions.

Miley, O'Melia, and DuBois (1995) conclude that the following issues must be an integral part of the advocacy process aimed at social injustice and social change:

1. The location of the problem must be identified. It must be determined, for example, whether the problem reflects a personal need, a gap in services, or inequitable social policy.

2. The objectives of intervention must be identified. For instance, objectives might be defined as procuring entitlements for clients or expanding job opportunities for oppressed individuals.

3. The target system of advocacy intervention must be identified. This at times might be the practitioner's own agency or other systems the agency works with.

4. The advocate must determine what authority or sanction he or she has to intervene in a targeted system. This can include legal rights of clients and judicial decisions.

5. The resources available for advocacy efforts must be identified. These resources include professional expertise, political influence, and one's credibility and reputation.

6. The degree to which the target system is receptive to the proposed advocacy effort must be determined. The target system will make this decision based on the reasonableness or lawfulness of the advocacy effort.

7. The level at which the intervention will occur must be analyzed to ensure that the desired outcomes will be achieved. Different levels of intervention might include policy changes, modification

of administrative procedures, and alterations in the discretionary actions taken by staff or management in an agency.

8. The object of intervention must be identified. This might include individual delivery services, agency administrators, or a legislative body.

9. The strategies of advocacy intervention must be determined. These strategies include the roles of negotiator, collaborator, and adversary.

10. Those involved in advocacy efforts must learn from the failures and successes of prior advocacy efforts.

What should be clear from the above information is the degree to which it is consistent with a social justice approach to practice. Furthermore, the above points suggest that advocacy is a holistic approach to social change that involves efforts at the micro and macro levels (Pardeck, 1996).

Those who are involved in advocacy efforts must understand the need for this type of intervention with the various systems they work with (Pardeck, 1996). It must be understood, if one considers the plight of people with disabilities, that public and private entities did not ask for the passage of the Americans With Disabilities Act. Most systems in the public and private sectors, including schools and businesses, would prefer self-regulation over a federal mandate aimed at protecting people with disabilities. Those involved in advocacy find that self-regulation does not work and that even after the passage of legislation such as the Americans With Disabilities Act, social systems mandated to conform to this law will attempt to avoid their legal obligations. This means advocacy is an absolute necessity to ensure that laws such as the ADA are implemented appropriately (Pardeck, 1996).

There are a number of reasons that entities legally bound by the mandates of civil rights legislation such as the ADA attempt to avoid compliance. First, organizations, including schools and private businesses, have been provided the compliance materials for the Americans With Disabilities Act; however, they often do not follow procedures set forth in compliance materials because they may contradict the bureaucratic rules of these systems. For example, the person with a disability brings a unique set of needs to the workplace, including the need at times for reasonable accommodations. Bureaucratic organizations are often rigid systems and are not prone to make exceptions; they must be forced to make exceptions through strong advocacy efforts (Pardeck, 1996).

Second, all public and private entities bound by the ADA feel that they operate on limited resources. If an employee with a disability requests a reasonable accommodation in order to do his or her job, the organization understands this to be an added cost. Advocates must persuade organizations asked to accommodate people with disabilities that this is a requirement of the law, and that the federal mandate for providing reasonable accommodations is based on the needs of the person with a disability and not on the needs of the organization's budget (Pardeck, 1996).

Third, people are often intimidated by public and private bureaucracies. For example, a person with a disability may have limited experience in and exposure to dealing with organizations in general. Such persons need the help of an expert, the advocate, in dealing with complex organizations. Skillful advocates understand how complex organizations work and are well aware of the regulations these systems must follow, including disability laws (Pardeck, 1996).

Last, it is often difficult for persons with disabilities to look at their problems objectively. Skillful advocates are able to step back from situations that negatively affect persons with disabilities and provide reason and objectivity to the process for both the person with a disability and the entity that is not complying with the ADA (Pardeck, 1996).

With the ADA as an example, the importance of advocacy even after a law has been passed to protect a category of people becomes clear. Advocacy is about influence and power, ingredients that are often critical to forcing entities to conform to regulations and laws (Pardeck, 1996).

EFFECTIVE ADVOCACY SKILLS FOR PERSONS WITH DISABILITIES

The ADA and other disability laws were enacted to protect the rights of people with disabilities; the history of the ADA suggests that persons with disabilities played a critical role in the creation of this law (Pardeck and Chung, 1992). People with disabilities have the primary responsibility of ensuring that their rights are met under the ADA. This can be achieved only if persons with disabilities learn to effectively advocate for themselves. The following strategies and skills are designed to help persons with disabilities become effective advocates for themselves. The goals of the following are to empower persons with disabilities to achieve social justice for themselves and others with disabilities.

Believing in Their Rights

Persons with disabilities must be taught that they are equal partners with others, such as professional social workers, who are involved with advocacy efforts. Equal partnership means that a person with a disability must accept his or her share of responsibility for solving problems related to advocacy efforts.

Having a Clear Vision

Persons with disabilities must learn to communicate clearly with systems that are denying them their rights under the ADA. They must be optimistic about what can be achieved as a result of advocacy. While trying to achieve what is perceived as ideal, they must be able to recognize what is realistic.

Organization

Persons with disabilities must understand that being organized is an absolute necessity to effective advocacy. They must know how to file information, keep track of records, and organize important documentation critical to the advocacy process. The person with a disability should be encouraged to date all materials and to make duplicate copies of all documents.

Prioritizing

Persons with disabilities must develop skills in learning to decide what the most important issues are related to their advocacy efforts. This should be based on their greatest needs as a person with a disability. One useful technique for prioritizing needs is to write them down on paper and prioritize them in order of importance.

Understanding One's Disabilities

A person with a disability must learn everything possible about his or her disability. It is important to acquire in-depth information about one's medical needs and the various assistive technology available as possible reasonable accommodations in the workplace or other settings. In general, persons with disabilities often know more than professionals about their special needs. It is important for a person with a disability to share information about his or her disability with the entity that is denying that person rights under the ADA. This information may help in the resolution of the problem between the person with a disability and an unresponsive system.

Knowing the Law

Persons with disabilities must learn about their rights under the ADA. They also should become familiar with their rights under other federal disability laws. By knowing these laws, they will be better able to advocate for their rights.

Following the Chain of Command

It is important for a person with a disability to know that effective advocacy means he or she should first engage those persons that can correct a problem at the lower levels of an organization. These individuals should be allowed the opportunity to address issues before the person with a disability moves to higher levels of organizations. If results cannot be obtained at a lower level, the individual with a disability must move systematically up the chain of command.

Being Informative

The person with a disability must understand his or her special needs. He or she should be able to convey all relevant information about his or her disability to the system at which advocacy efforts are aimed. This strategy can be helpful in resolving the problem between the person with a disability and the system denying the person's rights under the ADA.

Offering Solutions

The person with a disability needs to be creative in finding solutions to problems that call for advocacy efforts. Positive solutions are those that benefit everyone involved in the advocacy process. This kind of strategy can mean a successful resolution to the advocacy process.

Being Principled and Persistent

It is important for a person with a disability to master the art of being clear to officials about needed changes; one must be firm on these changes. It is important to keep at the advocacy process and not to let the battle become the issue. The person with a disability must avoid being adversarial and realize that he or she must be assertive and not aggressive. One must have a vision that the issue will be resolved to his or her satisfaction. It is best to assume that the system one is aiming advocacy efforts toward has honorable intentions.

Learning to Communicate Effectively

A person with a disability must understand that many problems result from poor communication between parties. It is important to learn to listen to what others are saying and to realize that others may have valuable insights into a problem. If a person with a disability does not understand something, he or she must ask questions. It is important to be sincere and honest, and to say what is really meant. Effective communication involves smiling and being relaxed, and not making others defensive. It is a good idea for a person with a disability to follow up conversations and meetings with a written summary of the discussion and agreements made.

Letting Others Know When Pleased

It is important to let the system that has changed because of advocacy efforts hear the person's satisfaction and excitement as the system progresses in implementing ADA rights. This kind of positive behavior will help keep the organization on the right track in disability law.

Developing Endurance

One of the first lessons learned from doing advocacy is that it is important to learn to develop endurance. Advocacy is a process that often extends over a long period. The person with a disability will face many challenges and issues; some successes and some failures need to be expected. It is important to learn lessons from both. The person with a disability must realize that if he or she has been successful in advocacy, for example, with an employer, that his or her relationship is likely to be long term with that employer. Effective advocacy skills will help make this relationship a positive one.

Following Through

One must make a concerted effort to monitor what has been agreed to as a result of the advocacy process. The person with a disability must make sure the accommodation or program changes are being provided appropriately. If the need for a different accommodation emerges, it is critical to advocate for these changes.

Having a Sense of Humor

Advocacy is about endurance. Cultivating a sense of humor is one of the most important traits a person with a disability needs for successful advocacy.

CONCLUSIONS

Advocacy is a powerful strategy for bringing about social change. It is an intervention strategy grounded in a social justice perspective. Advocacy is aimed at bringing about changes in social systems that deny people their basic rights; it is also aimed at expanding opportunities of the oppressed (Alinsky, 1946). Advocacy is a powerful role for changing the social environments of clients, including the systems that prevent individual growth and development. Advocacy is a critical role for those who wish to effectively bring about social change.

Even though there are numerous civil rights laws in place, including the Americans With Disabilities Act, public and private entities often attempt to avoid compliance with these laws. Civil rights laws are at times not followed because they contradict bureaucratic rules of organizations, and organizations often perceive these laws as contributing to added costs. When systems fail to comply with civil rights law, advocacy is a useful strategy for forcing them to comply.

This chapter offers strategies for empowering persons with disabilities through advocacy efforts. Even though advocacy is a highly technical skill, it is a skill that needs to be acquired by oppressed people. Advocacy is particularly effective when professionals teach people with disabilities how to advocate for themselves. Approaches for this kind of advocacy have been presented in this chapter.

REFERENCES

Alinsky, S. D. (1946). *Reveille for radicals.* Chicago: University of Chicago Press.

Brothwell, D. S., and Sandison, A. T. (1967). *Diseases in antiquity.* Springfield, IL: Charles C. Thomas.

Burgdorf, R. L., and Burgdorf, M. P. (1977). The wicked witch is almost dead: *Buck v. Bell* and the sterilization of handicapped persons. *Temple Law Quarterly* 50: 995–1054.

Federal Register. (1980). No. 66. Washington, DC: U.S. Government Printing Office.

Fiedler, L. (1978). *Freaks.* New York: Simon and Schuster.

Ianacone, B. P. (1977). Historical overview: From charity to rights. *Temple Law Quarterly* 50: 953–960.

Karger, H. J., and Stoesz, D. (1994). *American social welfare: A pluralist approach* (2nd ed). White Plains, NY: Longman.

Lewis, E. (1992). Social change and citizen action: A philosophical exploration for modern social group work. *Social Work With Groups* 14: 23–34.

McGowan, B. G. (1987). Advocacy. In A. Minahan (ed.), *Encyclopedia of social work: Vol. 1* (18th ed., pp. 89–95). Silver Spring, MD: National Association of Social Workers.

Miley, K. K., O'Melia, M., and DuBois, B. (1995). *Generalist social work practice: An empowering approach.* Boston: Allyn and Bacon.

Pardeck, J. T. (1996). *Social work practice: An ecological approach.* Westport: CT: Auburn House.

————. (1994, July/August). What you need to know about the Americans With Disabilities Act. *Coping*: 16–17.

Pardeck, J. T., and Chung, W. (1992). An analysis of the Americans With Disabilities Act of 1990. *Journal of Health and Social Policy*, 4: 47–56.

Rees, S. (1991). *Achieving power: Practice and policy in social welfare.* North Sydney, Australia: Allen & Unwin.

Chapter 7

ADA: Taking Stock and Looking to the Future

The ADA prohibits discrimination against persons with disabilities in the area of employment, public services and accommodations, transportation, and telecommunications. The ADA was enacted to provide a comprehensive national mandate for the elimination of discrimination against persons with disabilities in many aspects of American life.

The ADA evolved from two civil rights laws: the Civil Rights Act of 1964, and the Rehabilitation Act of 1973. In many ways the ADA is similar to these two laws. For example, the Civil Rights Act of 1964 prohibits discrimination on the basis of race, sex, religion, and national origin. The Rehabilitation Act prohibits discrimination based on disability; however, it covers only public and private entities receiving federal funds. The ADA, like the Rehabilitation Act, also prohibits discrimination on the basis of disabilities. The ADA is far more extensive than the Rehabilitation Act because it covers entities receiving federal funds and those that do not, such as private businesses. The ADA does more than simply adding disability to the list of protected classes because it requires public and private entities to provide reasonable accommodations to people with disabilities. No other protected class has this kind of right under civil rights law.

The ADA calls for attitudinal changes toward people with disabilities. An entirely new language, in fact, has emerged to describe persons with disabilities. For example, the word "handicapped" is now deemed inappropriate for describing a person with a disability. Many stereotypes are now being challenged by the disabilities rights movement. Persons with disabilities no longer want simply to receive subsidies from the government; they want to work. The employment rate of people with disabilities has been persistently low for the past 20 years; the ADA is attempting to alter this. For this to happen, however, many attitudes and stereotypes about people with disabilities must change.

As illustrated in this book, the ADA is a complicated law. Social workers must be particularly knowledgeable of the ADA because they have a tradition of working with people with disabilities and have long been advocates for oppressed people. Once social workers understand and learn the requirements under the ADA, the possibilities for doing advocacy work for people with disabilities become endless. Nearly all aspects of American life are affected by the ADA. Title I covers employment. Titles II and III prohibit discrimination on the basis of disabilities in virtually every service or program offered by public and private entities. Given the complexity of the rules governing the ADA, and the far-reaching nature of this new law, it will probably take decades for the ADA to be fully implemented in the public and private sectors. As shown in this book, employers who failed to implement the employment provisions under Title I of the ADA have paid millions of dollars to job applicants and employees whose rights were violated based on disability. The ADA is still a new law; social workers and American society in general have much to learn about the act.

One of the fascinating issues related to the ADA is that approximately one-half of persons with disabilities do not realize they are protected by this law (Shapiro, 1993). Once those with disabilities learn about their rights under the ADA, they will surely pressure the public and private sectors to fully implement the ADA's requirements.

DEFINING DISABILITY

One of the complex aspects of the ADA is the law's definition of a disability. Many stereotypes about the way disabilities have been traditionally understood are challenged by the definition of a disability under the ADA. Most people, including social workers, view disabilities as physical impairments that are obvious to able persons. Under the ADA, a disability is a far more complex phenomenon, because it includes having a record of an impairment and being regarded as having an impairment. For many people, the second and third prongs of the definition of a disability under the ADA are difficult to understand. However, if one has been discriminated against in employment because of a history of cancer or an emotional disability, the second prong of the definition, a record of an impairment, makes perfect sense. The employee who has been fired based on the belief that he or she has AIDS is well aware of why being regarded as having an impairment is the critical third part of defining a disabling condition.

Even those who understand the meaning of a disability under the ADA may be confused about why it is a violation under the ADA to ask questions about a person's disability during a job interview. Furthermore, social work faculty who screen students for admissions to social work programs are probably confused about whether they can ask an applicant about his or her disability during the admissions process. Students applying to social work programs, like job applicants, have a right under the ADA to keep their disabilities confidential unless they wish to share this information with an admissions committee or employer. In an educational setting, once the need for a reasonable accommodation is revealed by a student, faculty and other students still do not have a right under the ADA to know what kind of disability a student has who requests special assistance. Under this law, the faculty member is required to provide the reasonable accommodation; the student's disability remains confidential unless the student wishes to reveal it to the faculty member. These kinds of requirements present new challenges for social workers in virtually every practice setting.

TRAINING AND THE ADA

An effective strategy for better helping people under the ADA is to conduct training on the provisions of this law. Training is particularly critical for those who screen and hire job applicants. It is also important for those who work with people with disabilities to understand the ADA. In fact, people in virtually every setting in American life can benefit from training on the ADA.

The law's definition of a disability will require a great deal of training for people who work in human resources. This information is also critical to co-workers of people with disabilities. As mentioned previously, this definition is extremely complex. It is often hard for employees to not be inquisitive about a co-worker who receives reasonable accommodations. The ADA requires that the person's disability must remain confidential and only a few people in the workplace have a right to know his or her impairment. Training for employees will help them to better understand why the ADA requires almost total confidentiality concerning a person's disability in the work environment.

Reasonable accommodation is also a complex ADA requirement. Employees and supervisors, in particular, should be taught that most reasonable accommodations are inexpensive. They must also know that each request for a reasonable accommodation is considered on a case-by-case basis. Some employees may be required to help implement the accommodation for a fellow employee; training will help them do a better job of assisting a fellow worker with a disability.

It is also critical to include sensitivity training on how to interact with people with disabilities. For example, a person who is receiving treatment for cancer does not want fellow employees continually asking him or her about how the treatment is going. The person will share such information when he or she feels it is appropriate. Sensitivity training will also help able people understand the unique needs and problems of the person with a disability. The goal of such training should be to help eliminate stereotypes about and prejudices toward people with disabilities. Fersh and Thomas (1993: 130) offer some excellent points that can be used in sensitivity training. These are:

1. Separate the individual from the disability.

2. Recognize that persons with disabilities have rights, including privacy.

3. Treat individuals with disabilities with respect.

4. Avoid stereotyping individuals with disabilities by occupation or attribute; for example, "That's a disabled job," or "The mail room is the mentally retarded office."

Sensitivity training should emphasize that nondisabled people can do certain things to people with disabilities that can be perceived as demeaning and inappropriate. The able person may not intend to be inappropriate; however, his or her action may be seen as rude or patronizing by the person with a disability. Sensitivity training can help prevent this kind of behavior in the workplace as well as in other settings.

THE CIVIL RIGHTS ACT OF 1991 AND THE ADA

The Civil Rights Act of 1991 greatly strengthens the ADA because it allows plaintiffs who prevail to collect compensatory and punitive damages. The Civil Rights Act of 1991 also allows ADA plaintiffs to receive a jury trial. Compensatory damages include actual monetary losses, future monetary losses, and compensation for mental anguish and inconvenience. Compensatory damages have also been made available to persons with disabilities who have sued for employment discrimination under Section 504 of the Rehabilitation Act of 1973 (Fersh and Thomas, 1993).

Punitive damages are also available in cases of intentional discrimination. This means that if an employer intentionally discriminates against a person with a disability, punitive damages can be a remedy. The total award of punitive and compensatory damages for emotional distress and future monetary losses for an individual with a disability is limited by the size of the place of employment. For example, employers with fifteen to 100 employees have a limit of $50,000. Employers with 500 or more employees have a limit of $300,000. Under the Civil Rights Act of 1991, this cap applies to discrimination against all protected classes excluding discrimination based on race. One important aspect of the 1991 Civil Rights Act is that punitive damages are not available from state and local governments, even if intentional discrimination has occurred. Finally, no employer will be subjected to compensatory or punitive damages for failing to provide reasonable accommodation to a qualified person with a disability if the employer can demonstrate that good-faith efforts were made to provide the accommodation (Fersh and Thomas, 1993).

The Civil Rights Act of 1991 adds teeth to the ADA. It also means that an organization can be penalized if the ADA is violated. Fersh and Thomas (1993) suggest that gradually the caps for compensatory and punitive damages will be lifted; when this happens, the need for compliance with the ADA will become even greater.

THE FAMILY AND MEDICAL LEAVE ACT (FMLA)

FMLA is another federal act that in many ways complements the ADA because it affects families that have members with health care-related problems. Under FMLA, a full-time employee can have up to twelve weeks of unpaid, job-protected leave during a twelve-month period for the following reasons:

1. To care for a newborn child, a newly adopted child, or a child who has been placed in foster care in an employee's home.

2. To care for a child, parent, or spouse who has a serious health problem.

3. For an employee's own serious health problem.

FMLA went into effect in August 1993, and applies to any employer with fifty or more employees. The United States Department of Labor is responsible for the implementation of the Family and Medical Leave Act.

NEW HEALTH INSURANCE LEGISLATION

The Health Insurance Portability and Accountability Act (HIPAA)(1996) also has tremendous implications for people with disabilities. This law should help decrease discrimination in employment for people with disabilities because it mandates that people with health conditions will not lose their health insurance coverage because of job loss, illness, or changing of jobs. As noted earlier, people with a history of serious illness have traditionally been denied or fired from jobs because employers fear these individuals will increase the cost of health care benefits. Even though such actions are illegal under the ADA, the Health Insurance Portability and Accountability Act will give employers less incentive for this kind of behavior.

The Health Insurance Portability and Accountability Act will also help people with disabilities move to new employment opportunities. Millions of people with health conditions have been locked into jobs they may not like because if they changed employment, they would lose their health care insurance. This law allows an employee with a health condition to continue his or her coverage when changing jobs. If a person was covered for twelve months or more in his previous job, that person will have uninterrupted coverage upon taking a new position or with individual coverage. Self-employed persons who can pay the health insurance premiums will also have the same opportunities. Another part of this law is a four-year, market-driven experiment for tax-sheltered Medical Savings Accounts for 750,000 employed persons under the age of sixty-five.

POSITIVE INDICATORS AND FUTURE TRENDS

Even though there continues to be high unemployment and underemployment among people with disabilities, many have benefited from the ADA. For example, the EEOC has intervened on behalf of many people with disabilities who have been discriminated against in the workplace. The Department of Justice and Department of Education have both been active in helping to ensure compliance with Title II. There are many people with disabilities who are highly educated and earn excellent incomes. The ADA and other similar federal legislation have helped these individuals in their pursuit of equal opportunity in the workplace.

Advances in assistive technology have played an important role in enhancing the employability of people with disabilities. Communication devices have been developed that enable an individual without speech to talk. Computer technology can help people without fine motor control to write. Assistive-listening devices have been developed that improve communication for individuals with hearing impairments. These kinds of devices are effectively being used as reasonable accommodations for people with impairments in the workplace and in educational settings.

Many employers have reported that the implementation of the ADA has been relatively smooth in most aspects of the workplace. Meisinger (1984) notes that the process used to implement the ADA has helped employers learn about their obligations in advance, and many feel comfortable with their new obligations to people with disabilities. Employers are finding that persons with disabilities are as good as or better than able workers (Pardeck, 1994).

The evidence suggests that the educational level of people with disabilities as a whole remains low. A Harris (1994) survey found, however, that their educational levels are improving. For example, the poll found that 44 percent of adults with disabilities had completed some college or received a college degree, compared with 30 percent in 1986. In time, these trends will be reflected in the work force.

Clearly, the ADA is having a significant impact on all aspects of American life. Even though the federal government has been implementing a number of laws over the last several decades that improved opportunities for people with disabilities, the ADA is the capstone of these efforts. Many of the prior laws affecting people with disabilities have been paternalistic. The ADA is not that kind of law because it is aimed at increasing self-sufficiency among people with disabilities and their full participation in the workplace.

In a sense, the past paternalistic legislation aimed at people with disabilities is a contradiction to the ADA. These older laws, like welfare programs in general, have built-in requirements that penalize individuals with disabilities who wish to work. For example, it is irrational for a person with a disability to take a low-paying job that lacks health insurance benefits over a government-supported program that includes such benefits. Unfortunately, many of the federal support programs provide very low payments, which means a life of poverty for persons with disabilities. Strategies need to be developed that help ensure that people with disabilities do not have to make choices that are equally negative.

The ADA is slowly doing its job. It has had a notable impact on the lives of people with disabilities. In a sense, the ADA has started a slow evolutionary process that will gradually change American life for the better. Just as the Civil Rights Act of 1964 changed lives for the better for people of color and other minorities, the ADA will have a similar impact on persons with disabilities. There is, however, still much to be done in the area of disability policy.

REFERENCES

Fersh, D., and Thomas, P. W. (1993). *Complying with the Americans with Disabilities Act.* Westport, CT: Quorum Books.

Harris, L. and Associates (1994). *NOD/Harris survey of Americans with disabilities.* Washington, DC: National Organization on Disabilities.

Meisinger, S. (1994). *Statement of the society for human resource management before U.S. Commission on Civil Rights.* Washington, DC: United States Commission on Civil Rights.

Pardeck, J. T. (1994, July/August). What you need to know about the Americans With Disabilities Act. *Coping:* 16–17.

Shapiro, J. P. (1993). *No pity: People with disabilities forging a new civil rights movement.* New York: Times Books.

Appendix

A Brief Overview of the Americans With Disabilities Act

The following summary is based on *A Guide to Disability Rights Laws* (U.S. Department of Justice, 1996). This summary provides basic information on the Americans with Disabilities Act of 1990.

The ADA prohibits discrimination on the basis of disability in employment, state and local government, public accommodations, commercial facilities, transportation, and telecommunications. It also applies to the U.S. Congress.

To be protected by the ADA, one must have a disability or have a relationship or association with an individual with a disability. An individual with a disability is defined by the ADA as a person who has a physical or mental impairment that substantially limits one or more major life activities, a person who has a history or record of such an impairment, or a person who is perceived by others as having such an impairment. The ADA does not specifically name all of the impairments that are covered, but it does list those conditions that are not covered.

ADA TITLE I: EMPLOYMENT

Title I requires employers with fifteen or more employees to provide qualified individuals with disabilities an equal opportunity to benefit from the full range of employment-related opportunities available to others. For example, it prohibits discrimination in recruitment, hiring, promotions, training, pay, social activities, and other privileges of employment. It restricts questions that can be asked about an applicant's disability before a job offer is made and it requires that employers make reasonable accommodations to the known physical or mental limitations of otherwise qualified individuals with disabilities, unless doing so results in undue hardship. Religious entities with fifteen or more employees are covered under Title I.

Title I complaints must be filed with the U.S. Equal Employment Opportunity Commission (EEOC) within 180 days of the date of discrimination, or within 300 days if the charge is filed with a designated or local fair-employment practice agency. Individuals may file suit in federal court only after they receive a "right-to-sue" letter from the EEOC.

Charges of employment discrimination on the basis of disability may be filed at any EEOC field office. Field offices are located in fifty cities throughout the United States and are listed in most telephone directories under "U.S. Government."

ADA TITLE II: STATE AND LOCAL GOVERNMENT ACTIVITIES

Title II covers all activities of state and local governments regardless of the government entity's size or receipt of federal funding. Title II requires that state and local government give people with disabilities an equal opportunity to benefit from all of their programs, services, and activities (e.g., public education, employment, transportation, recreation, health care, social services, courts, voting, and town meetings).

State and local governments are required to follow specific architectural standards in the construction and alteration of their buildings. They also must relocate programs or otherwise provide access in inaccessible older buildings, and communicate effectively with people who have hearing, vision, or speech disabilities. Public entities are not required to take actions that would result in undue financial and administrative burdens. They are required to make reasonable modifications to policies, practices, and procedures where necessary to avoid discrimination unless they can demonstrate that doing so would fundamentally alter the nature of the service, program, or activity being provided.

Complaints of Title II violation may be filed with the Department of Justice within 180 days of the date of discrimination. In certain situations, cases may be referred to a mediation program sponsored by the department. The department may bring suit where it has investigated a matter and has been unable to resolve violations.

Title II may also be enforced through private lawsuits in federal court. It is not necessary to file a Title II complaint with the Department of Justice or other federal agency, or to receive a "right-to-sue" letter, before going to court.

ADA TITLE II: PUBLIC TRANSPORTATION

The transportation provisions of Title II cover public transportation services, such as city buses and public rail transit (e.g. subways, commuter rails, Amtrak). Public transportation authorities may not discriminate against people with disabilities in the provision of their services. They must comply with requirements for accessibility in newly purchased vehicles, make good-faith efforts to purchase or lease accessible used buses, remanufacture buses in an accessible manner, and unless it would result in an undue burden, provide paratransit where they operate fixed-route or rail systems. Paratransit is a service in which individuals who are unable to use the regular transit system independently (because of a physical or mental impairment) are picked up and dropped off at their destinations. Questions and complaints about transportation must be directed to the Federal Transit Administration, U.S. Department of Transportation.

ADA TITLE III: PUBLIC ACCOMMODATIONS

Title III covers businesses and nonprofit service providers for public accommodations, privately operated entities offering certain types of courses and examinations, privately operated transportation, and commercial facilities. Public accommodations are private entities that own, lease, lease to, or operate facilities such as restaurants, retail stores, hotels, movie theaters, private schools, convention centers, doctors' offices, homeless shelters, transportation depots, zoos, funeral homes, day care centers, and recreation facilities including sports stadiums and fitness clubs. Transportation services provided by private entities are also covered by Title III.

Public accommodations must comply with basic nondiscrimination requirements that prohibit exclusion, segregation, and unequal treatment. They must comply with requirements related to architectural standards for new and altered buildings: reasonable modifications to policies, practices, and procedures; effective communication with people with hearing, vision, or speech disabilities; and other access requirements. Additionally, public accommodations must remove barriers in buildings where it is easy to do so without much difficulty or expense, given the public accommodation's resources.

Courses and examinations related to professional, educational, or trade-related applications, licensing, certifications, or credentialing must be provided in a place and manner accessible to people with disabilities, or alternative accessible arrangements must be offered.

Commercial facilities, such as factories and warehouses, must comply with the ADA's architectural standards for new construction and alteration.

Complaints of Title III violations may be filed with the Department of Justice. Certain cases may be referred to a mediation program sponsored by the department. The department is authorized to sue where there is a pattern or practice of discrimination in violation of Title III, or where an act of discrimination raises an issue of general public importance. Title III may also be enforced through private lawsuits. It is not necessary to file a Title III complaint with the Department of Justice (or any federal agency) or to receive a "right-to-sue" letter before going to court.

ADA TITLE IV: TELECOMMUNICATIONS

Title IV addresses telephone and television access for people with hearing and speech disabilities. It requires common carriers (telephone companies) to establish interstate and intrastate telecommunications relay services (TRS) twenty-four hours a day, seven days a week. TRS enables callers with hearing and speech disabilities who use text telephones (TTYs or TDDs), and callers who use voice telephones, to communicate with each other through a third-party communications assistant. The Federal Communications Commission (FCC) has set minimum standards for TRS services. Title IV requires closed captioning of federally funded public service announcements.

REFERENCE

U.S. Department of Justice. (1996). *A guide to disabilities rights laws.* Washington, DC: Government Printing Office.

Sources for Further Reading

Adaptive Environments Center, Inc. (1992). *ADA Title II action guide*. Horsham, PA: Axon Group Company.

Bennett-Alexander, D. L. & Pincus, L. B. (1985). *Employment law for business*. Chicago, IL: Irwin.

Cole, B. S., Christ, C. C., & Light, T. R. (1995). Social work education and students with disabilities: Implications of Section 504 and the ADA. *Journal of Social Work Education*, 31, 261–268.

Fersh, D., & Thomas, P. W. (1993). *Complying with the Americans With Disabilities Act*. Westport, CT: Quorum Books.

Fiedler, J. F. (1994). *Mental disabilities and the Americans With Disabilities Act: A concise compliance manual for executives*. Westport, CT: Quorum Books.

Gordon, E. B. (1994). Promoting the relevance of policy to practice: Using the ADA to teach social policy. *Journal of Teaching in Social Work*, 10, 165–176.

Harris, L. & Associates. *NOD/Harris Survey of Americans With Disabilities*. Washington, D.C.: National Organization on Disabilities.

Harrison, M. & Gilbert, S. (eds.) (1992). *The Americans With Disabilities Act Handbook*. Beverly Hills, CA: Excellent Books.

Kearney, D. S., Green, M., & Walter, P. H. (eds.) (1992). *The new ADA: Compliance and costs*. Kingston, MA: R. S. Means Company.

Kopels, S. (1995). The Americans with Disabilities Act: A tool to combat poverty. *Journal of Social Work Education*, 31, 337–346.

McEntree, M. K. (1995). Deaf and hard-of-hearing clients: Some legal implications. *Social Work*, 40, 183–187.

Morrissey, P. A. (1993). *The educator's guide to the Americans with Disabilities Act*. Alexandria, VA: The American Vocational Association.

Moxley, D. (1992). Disability policy and social work practice. *Health and Social Work*, 17, 99–103.

Orlin, M. (1995). The Americans with Disabilities Act: Implications for social services. *Social Work*, 40, 233–239.

Pardeck, J. T. (1994, July/August). What you need to know about the Americans with Disabilities Act. *Coping,* 16–17.

Pardeck, J. T. (1997). Americans with Disabilities Act of 1990: Implications for human services agencies. *The Clinical Supervisor*, 15, 147–161.

Pardeck, J. T., & Chung, W. S. (1992). An analysis of the Americans with Disabilities Act of 1990. *Journal of Health and Social Policy*, 4, 47–56.

Perritt, H. H. (1991). *Americans with Disabilities Act handbook*. New York: Wiley Law Publications.

Quinn, P. (1995). Social work education and disability: Benefiting from the impact of the ADA. *Journal of Teaching in Social Work*, 12, 55–71.

Raines, J. B., & Rossow, L. F. (1994). The Americans with Disabilities Act: Resolving the separate-but-equal problem in colleges and universities. *West's Education Law Reporter*, 88, 1–11.

Sales, B. D., & VandenBos, G. R. (eds.) (1994). *Psychology in litigation and legislation*. Washington, DC: American Psychological Association.

Shapiro, J. P. (1993). *No pity: People with disabilities forging a new civil rights movement*. New York: Times Books.

Taylor, B., & Taylor, A. (1996). Social work with transport disabled persons: A way finding perspective in health care. *Social Work in Health Care*, 23, 3–19.

Veres, J. G., and Sims, R. R. (eds.) (1995). *Human resources management and the Americans with Disabilities Act*. Westport, CT: Quorum Books.

Woody, R. H. (1993). Americans with Disabilities Act: Implications for family therapy. *American Journal of Family Therapy*, 21, 71–78.

Index

About the Author

JOHN T. PARDECK is Professor of Social Work at Southwest Missouri State University. He has published extensively on the topic of human services.